Planning for Contact in Permanent Placements

Paul Adams

BAAF
ADOPTION
& FOSTERING

Published by
British Association for Adoption & Fostering
(BAAF)
Saffron House
6-10 Kirby Street
London EC1N 8TS
www.baaf.org.uk

Charity registration 275689 (England and Wales) and SC039337 (Scotland)
© BAAF, 2012

British Library Cataloguing in Publication Data
A catalogue record for this book is available from the British Library

ISBN 978 1 907585 51 7

Project management by Shaila Shah, Director of Publications, BAAF
Designed and typeset by Helen Joubert Design
Printed in Great Britain by the Lavenham Press

BAAF is the leading UK-wide membership organisation for all those concerned with adoption, fostering and child care issues.

Contents

1	**Introduction and context**	**1**
	Introduction	1
	Definitions	3
	Historical context	4
	Current data	6
2	**The purpose of contact in permanence**	**7**
	Identity and permanence	7
	Purpose of contact	10
3	**Research evidence**	**15**
	Introduction	15
	The need for openness and honesty	16
	Face-to-face contact can work well	16
	Face-to-face contact can also be problematic	18
	Indirect contact can work well but can be challenging	19
	No contact is right for some children	20
	The impact of social networking	21
	How much contact?	22
	Conclusion	23
4	**The legal framework**	**24**
	England and Wales	24
	Northern Ireland	27
	Scotland	29
5	**Assessment**	**36**
	Introduction	36
	The child	36
	The birth family	40
	The adopters or permanent foster carers	46

6 Myths and misunderstandings   **49**

7 Contact in kinship care   **55**
   introduction   55
   Research   55
   Implications   57
   Statutory guidance in England   58
   Assessing contact in kinship care   59

8 Conclusion   **62**
   The context   62
   The purpose of contact   62
   Assessment   63
   Kinship care   65
   The challenge   65

Appendix – Case studies   **66**
   Case study: Will, Chris and Neil   66
   Case study: Amanda and Debbie   68
   Case study: Bailey   70
   Case study: Alisha   72
   Case study: Tyler, Rosa and Jenna   74

Bibliography   **76**

Acknowledgements

I am grateful to the authors of the BAAF good practice guide on Contact in Permanence that was published in 1999; sections from that text have been carried forward where they continue to be relevant. My thanks also go to the BAAF legal leads for each UK country: Alexandra Conroy-Harris, Sarah Coldrick, Frances Nicholson, and Lexy Plumtree who effectively wrote the legal chapter between them.

While writing this book I have appreciated the advice and comments of a number of individuals including Berni Stringer (whose child-centred perspective was invaluable), Catherine Mullin, Frances Nicholson, Ravinder Kaur, David Roth and Pascale Davison. I thank them all for their time and encouragement, and acknowledge that the limitations of the final text are entirely my responsibility.

Shaila Shah and the BAAF publications team made some very helpful suggestions, and turned a manuscript into the finished article. Finally, I would like to thank John Simmonds for his wisdom and guidance – encouraging me to be less directive and more reflective – and for being a supportive manager in all respects.

Note about the author

Paul Adams qualified as a social worker in 1993, having been inspired by working as a foster carer in the US. He has worked predominantly in local authority children's services, managing child care and fostering teams.

Paul joined BAAF as a Fostering Development Consultant in 2010. He chairs both fostering and adoption panels, sits on GSCC registration and conduct committees, and provides consultancy and training. He has published research and co-authored a good practice guide on parent and child fostering.

He lives in North Wales with his partner Sarah, and rescue dogs Simba and Bluebell.

1

Introduction and context

INTRODUCTION

Planning contact in the context of permanence is a complex and challenging area for social workers, and there is anecdotal evidence to suggest that social workers often struggle with this aspect of their work. Local authorities, Health and Social Care Trusts in Northern Ireland,[1] and adoption and fostering agencies often have very different cultures around contact, and it is only the best informed practitioners who are confident in using research evidence to justify the contact plans they are making.

This practice guide is designed to assist social workers and managers in this difficult area, and replaces an older BAAF practice guide (Barker *et al*, 1999) that contained much useful information, but has become increasingly outdated. The guide is deliberately a short one. It aims to present the issues in a way that is easily accessible to hard-pressed social workers; and in so doing, leave them better placed to make informed decisions resulting in improved outcomes for children. It is a tool to inform practice and not an academic text.

If social workers who are making contact plans for children in the context of permanence are familiar with the ideas contained in this guide, they will be able to present well argued and reasoned justifications for the contact plans set out in written reports[2] including court reports. It is also hoped that this guide will help social workers feel more confident in recommending particular contact plans, and that they will feel better able to defend their positions under examination.

Readers do need to be clear about the limitations of this practice guide. It is focused very clearly on the making of contact plans as part of a permanence plan; it is not about implementing, supporting or reviewing these plans. It does not address questions about how written

---

1   Where local authorities are referenced in the remainder of this guide, this reference will include Health and Social Care Trusts in Northern Ireland where relevant.
2   In England this will usually be the Child's Permanence Report (CPR), in Wales the Child's Adoption Assessment Report (CAAR), and in Scotland and Northern Ireland the BAAF Form E.

contact plans should be constructed; how children, parents and others should be prepared for contact; where contact should take place; how supervision should be undertaken; whether contact should coincide with special times such as festivals and birthdays; or how letterbox services can be organised. These important questions are for elsewhere and not for this practice guide.

Neither does this guide offer any easy answers to questions about what contact plan is appropriate to any particular situation; on the contrary, a consistent theme is the importance of assessing individual circumstances, a task that demands time and effort in the context of good professional working relationships with children and families. There are no easy shortcuts in this work, although a well-informed and robust contact plan is less likely to be challenged, and so may save time, effort and delay in the long run.

It is important to be clear about the limitations of contact planning in permanence, and to understand that any agreed plan is only an initial plan that must be viewed as flexible and subject to changing needs and circumstances. It is impossible to accurately predict a child's contact needs for the long-term future because of all the potential variables that may arise over time, and so any identified plan must only be seen as a starting point and not a fixed arrangement for the duration of a child's minority.

Birth families need to understand that they have no "entitlement" in relation to having prescribed fixed arrangements if these arrangements cease to be appropriate; and adopters need to understand that contact levels might need to increase or decrease, or structurally change, depending on the child's changing needs. Some practitioners will argue that coming up with any meaningful plan prior to placement is impossible, but whatever the merits of this view, the courts will nevertheless usually require some indication about what is envisaged at the outset.

This guide is written primarily with children's social workers in mind; a tool to help them in planning contact for children moving to permanence. However, it will also be of interest to adoption and fostering workers who need to ensure that when assessing and preparing permanent carers, they are doing so with a good understanding of what children need. New permanent families must genuinely understand the benefits that can be achieved from contact for both them and their children, and also recognise that the contact plan will need to be seen as a starting point; something that must be subject to review and change.

The practice guide is structured in the following way. Chapter 1 sets out the history and context of contact, and Chapter 2 considers the purpose of contact in the context of a child moving to a new permanent family. Chapter 3 brings together the research evidence, and Chapter 4 looks at the legal context for each of the four countries of the UK. Chapter 5 looks at what should be considered when assessing and formulating a contact plan. Chapter 6 explores myths in contact planning, and Chapter 7 looks at contact in kinship placements before Chapter 8 brings together the various themes in a conclusion. An appendix provides some anonymised case studies based on real examples.

DEFINITIONS

Permanence

Although at times this practice guide might appear to emphasise adoption as the most common permanence arrangement, the issues discussed will apply in the range of legal frameworks for permanence, including permanent fostering and special guardianship.

Contact

The term *contact* encompasses different forms of direct and indirect communication between a child and his or her carers with a range of people including birth parents, siblings, extended family members and previous carers.

Direct contact is used primarily to mean face-to-face contact, but can also involve communication by letter, cards, telephone, email or through social networking media. The key issue is that the contact is directly between the child and the other person, whatever the medium for doing this.

Indirect contact describes any communication that involves going through a third party, usually the adoption agency. This is often described as letterbox contact, and can be used for the exchange of letters, cards, photographs and presents. There are some indications that in the near future communication through social networking media might also be managed through a third party, and so this could also potentially be indirect contact.

Openness

It is not possible to make sense of contact issues without a consideration and understanding of *openness* (Brodzinsky, 2005), a concept that is discussed throughout this guide. This term came to be used to describe situations that stressed a more inclusive and less secretive approach to contact issues in adoption. Some practitioners have used the term to refer to situations involving direct contact, but openness does not necessarily need to involve direct contact, and can be seen in both psychological and structural terms.

Structural openness most commonly refers to direct or indirect contact but could also include working closely with birth family members in relation to identifying appropriate adopters, exchanging information prior to placement, and a one-off introductory meeting between birth family and adopters.

Psychological openness describes a state of mind, often of adopters, where this openness is reflected in how they communicate with their child about the fact that he or she is adopted, and their sensitivity as to how that may feel for the child at different stages in their life. The term can apply equally to other permanence arrangements.

HISTORICAL CONTEXT

The historical context in relation to adoption and contact has been set out in a number of texts (Barker *et al*, 1999; MacCaskill, 2002; Neil and Howe, 2004; Smith and Logan, 2004; Young and Neil, 2009). Prior to the 1970s, adoption in the UK was primarily used to find families for healthy babies, and it was felt that a "clean break" from the past was best for both the child and the birth family. For the most part, these arrangements were characterised by secrecy and shame, and contact with birth family after adoption was extremely rare. It was believed that these "closed" adoptions would protect both the child and birth mother from the stigma of illegitimacy, and allow them both to move on without unhelpful interference from or thoughts about the past. During this period, toddlers and older children entering the care system were accommodated in foster care or residential homes, and were rarely considered for adoption.

The 1970s saw the emergence of the "permanence movement" that emphasised the need to promote adoption for older and otherwise "hard to place" children, that in some parts of the UK often meant black children. Older black children, who had hitherto been placed primarily with foster carers, were now being placed for adoption, usually with white families, and according to Weise (1987), 'permanence for the black child became synonymous with the concept of transracial adoption'.

In making adoption plans for older children, professionals tended to favour approaches to contact that had been hitherto applied to traditional baby adoptions, but the older children often had established relationships with their birth family, and were understandably reluctant to relinquish these. Furthermore, the severance of links with birth relatives and the wider community had an added dimension for transracially placed black children, and black parents and professionals began to challenge the dominant closed models of permanence, noting that inclusive approaches to permanence – usually in the form of kinship arrangements – were commonplace in non-Western societies.

Alongside these developments, researchers had already started to raise questions about the psychological needs of children living away from their birth families. Sants (1964) identified the 'genealogically bewildered child' as having no or uncertain knowledge about his or her biological parents, with an associated impact on identity formation. Triseliotis (1973) detailed the need for children in care to know about their origins, reflecting the emerging evidence from adopted adults who revealed that the closed models of adoption left them with unresolved questions about their family history, culture and identity. Rowe and Lambert (1973) emphasised the importance of contact with birth families as part of planning for the rehabilitation home of children who were in foster care or residential settings.

Contact emerged as a professional issue in this context, and by the 1980s there was a growing awareness of the need for more openness and less secrecy in adoption and permanence. It is significant that the Children Act 1989 in England and Wales, the Children (Scotland) Act 1995 and the Children (Northern Ireland) Order 1995, gave recognition to the importance of contact for children in care, and increased or clarified the rights of children, parents and other family members to seek contact.

Practice in the UK has also been influenced by practice and research from elsewhere, and by the 1990s the benefits of openness were evident in New Zealand and the US. Maori practices in New Zealand challenged the traditional assumptions about the need for secrecy in adoption practice; and practice in the US was indicating that more open adoption involving direct contact could work well for all parties (see Neil and Howe, 2004).

Probably the most significant development of the 2000s is the growth of social networking (Fursland, 2010) that makes it much easier for separated people to make contact with each other directly. For many adopted and fostered people this has been very positive, but it also means that birth parents and others can attempt to trace children in order to subvert any agreed contact plans, and curious children and young people can relatively easily locate members of their birth family outside of any agreed plans. This development has the potential for breaching confidentiality and allows for unexpected and unplanned contact, bringing anxiety and stress to all parties. This growth in social networking brings huge challenges to those planning contact in permanence and needs to be considered at all stages of the process.

CURRENT DATA

We do not have reliable data about the level and type of contact experienced by adopted children. *The Prime Minister's Review of Adoption* (Performance and Innovation Unit, 2000) for England and Wales used an estimate that 70 per cent of adopted children have some contact, either direct or indirect. Neil (2002), in a study of children placed when they were under four years of age, found that 89 per cent had plans for some sort of ongoing contact with their birth family, including 17 per cent with a plan that included direct contact with adult birth family members. Biehal *et al*'s (2010) study showed 15 per cent of adopted children were having face-to-face contact with a birth parent (often where children had been adopted by foster carers) and about half were having letterbox contact. Lowe *et al* (1999), who considered an older aged sample, found that 39 per cent of children were having direct contact with an adult birth family member. It is generally considered that contact levels between adopted siblings are higher than this.

In terms of permanent foster care, it is estimated that about 60 per cent of children have face-to-face contact with at least one birth parent (Cleaver, 2000; Neil and Howe, 2004) although a higher figure of 81 per cent is cited by Biehal *et al* (2010).

It is clear from these discussions that there has been a move from the traditional closed approach that characterised permanence pre-1970s, to a situation where the benefits of openness are now widely recognised; but which is also now seriously complicated by developments in social networking. The fact is that the vast majority of children in adoptive homes or in foster care will have some sort of ongoing contact with their birth family, and the challenge for practitioners is to make sure that when considering contact plans, they do this in a way that achieves the best possible outcomes for the individual children in each set of circumstances.

2
The purpose of contact in permanence

IDENTITY AND PERMANENCE

It is difficult to separate issues of identity and permanence. It is the fact of having two families, one born into and another one that the child is a full member of, that makes adopted and permanently fostered children feel different from other children. Making sense of two life narratives will impact on children and adopted adults in different ways but the identity of having two families cannot be separated from questions about contact.

> Contact can be defined as the symbolic representation of the young person's relationship with, at least, two sets of families. The type of contact, whether it is face-to-face or letterbox and all the many variations, carries a message about the nature of the relationship.
>
> (Lindsey, 2006, p 221)

Interviews conducted with adopted children (Thomas and Beckford, 1999) illustrate the complexity of issues that relate to contact and identity, often characterised by confusion and high levels of emotion.

> I don't know, sometimes I feel like not seeing them at all. Sometimes I have all sorts of feelings.
>
> (Wanda, quoted in Thomas and Beckford, 1999, p 95)

> Like sometimes when we see [my birth mum] you feel that you needed to cry when you leave her and things, but you hold it in to be brave for everyone else...I mean it's okay if you get used to holding your tears in, if you know you're going to see your mum again...
>
> (Janine, quoted in Thomas and Beckford, 1999, p 96)

Some children in the study felt an obligation to birth parents who were unwell; some remained angry at how they were treated. Others were simply inquisitive, wanting to know what their family looked like, how old their parents and siblings were and where they lived. Some expressed little interest in knowing about birth families because they felt their identity was established with their alternative families, but these children were in the minority, and for most, the complex and often difficult histories with birth families continued to impact on how they viewed themselves.

Verrier (2009) described the relationship between a child and its mother at birth as 'mystical, mysterious, spiritual and everlasting' and talks of the 'primal wound' that results from disrupting this relationship. She asserts that the breaking of a connection with the birth mother will have profound and lasting implications for any child, even where they were adopted at a very young age and there are no explicit memories of the birth mother. What is left is more than simply curiosity or a need for information but rather conscious or unconscious feelings of abandonment and incompleteness, feelings that are difficult to erase or ease – even in the most loving alternative home. While some adopted adults would not recognise the intensity of the "primal wound", for many this describes their experience in a way that is resonant for them.

What cannot be denied is the fact that every adopted person retains a separate biological identity that was formed before adoption and in a relationship that developed during the nine months of pregnancy (and often longer). A sense of being with another may exist alongside an emerging identity within a substitute permanent family. This may be further intensified if children have lived with birth parents for extended periods before being removed and an identity developed in a context characterised by abuse or neglect. This means that the majority of children adopted from care or permanently fostered will bring with them an existing identity, often combined with unresolved grief that comes from the circumstances that necessitated their permanent removal from the birth family.

Adopters and social workers need to understand this at an emotional and a cognitive level and understand why the "clean break" approach to adoption has been replaced by a model that requires all parties to engage with the emotional complexities and challenges that come with children moving into permanent substitute families. Adults need to retain a child-centred perspective; to recognise that with adoption will often come interest or curiosity about birth family, longings to meet them or return to them (even if there is also a recognition that this is undesirable). Unlike a bereavement – which has a sense of finality about it – the adopted or permanently fostered child's birth family will never go away and potentially their influence and the possibility of meeting will remain with the adopted child throughout life, with greater prominence at certain times.

The challenge for social workers is to "feel" what it means for the child to have two families, and to understand this with real empathy. They need to recognise that it is normal for a child to want to know about their family of origin, and that these feelings will likely be stronger at some times than others. Only then can they can plan contact in a way that recognises both the potential benefit as well as the potential threat to the child's emerging identity and maximise the opportunities for helping a child to manage their reality effectively.

In part, that will mean planning for questions *now and in the future*, and at the same time giving children the space and permission they need to be full and integrated members of their new families. It will also mean thinking about how children might use social networking sites to make contact with birth family, to be prepared for that, and to ensure that substitute carers are equally prepared. When children have experienced abuse, they will need help to make sense of that, to feel secure that the abuse has ended, and to be provided with an environment where they can develop the strategies and skills for functioning in a setting where adults are safe and trustworthy.

This brings us back to Brodzinsky (2005) and the idea of communicative openness, a concept that needs to be understood and practised by both adopters, foster carers, and social workers who are developing contact plans. Simmonds (2011, p 40) summarises what this means.

> The concept of "communicative openness" recognises that all the parties in adoption need to be able to think about, discuss and be generally open to all the issues that adoption stirs up – the facts and circumstances that led to the adoption, the people involved, the meaning it has to those people and the differences between them and how that changes over time. This needs to become woven into the lived experience of all those involved.

We need to understand that we are asking a lot of children and adopters to manage the identity issues that come with adoption or permanence; it is an emotionally challenging task, and one unique to the experience of being substitute carers. However, it is not something that can be avoided; it is integral to adoption and permanence, and needs to be dealt with.

This was always the case, but with the emergence of social networking it is even more vital that the issues are not ignored. All parties need to be prepared for the fact that children have an option to utilise technology to locate birth family if they decide to do so. In cases where it is absolutely necessary to prevent any direct contact for reasons of safety, it is imperative that children are clear about this, and have a shared understanding of the dangers. They will need to agree to play their part in keeping the family safe, and to achieve this will require a communicative openness between the child and the adopters or foster carers from the outset, so that where a child might be considering using social media, they feel able to discuss the implication of this with trusted and knowledgeable adults. They will also need to have been provided with honest and truthful information about the risk their birth family might pose.

In other less dangerous cases, social workers might need to recognise that efforts to prevent direct contact will in many cases be futile, and that many children will choose to make contact with birth family through social networking sites. There is no point in pretending that this won't happen, and the potential benefits of allowing managed and planned direct contact will need to be considered against the risks of ending up with unmediated contact initiated by the child.

Any contact plan will need to be subject to ongoing review, influenced by the impact of contact on the child's development in the context of the increasing sense of belonging with a family over time. However, this does not mean that plans can be left vague at the outset; this will not work for anyone. On the contrary, the complex issues discussed in this section highlight the importance of establishing a contact plan with a clear purpose, and with a structure that reflects this purpose. For social workers, the requirement, and the challenge, is to produce a clear contact plan, in a context involving numerous variables and unknowns.

PURPOSE OF CONTACT

It is widely agreed that maintaining or developing contact must provide a developmental benefit for the child; it has no inherent value in itself.

While writers tend to categorise the purpose of contact using a variety of different headings and sub-headings, they ultimately identify the same factors that can potentially benefit children in alternative permanent families. This practice guide, influenced by Neil and Howe (2004), sets out the key purposes of contact as follows:

1) **Enabling attachment to new carers** (by countering feelings of guilt, anxiety and self-blame, and by avoiding idealisation);

2) **Promoting positive identity** (by providing the child with genealogical and historical information);

3) **Enabling emotional healing and promoting self-esteem** (by dealing with loss, trauma and rejection).

These three aspects are most likely to be achieved in arrangements that are psychologically open, and ideally structurally open, although contact arrangements will serve different functions for different children, changing over time:

> Some children clearly had a huge emotional investment in the relationship. Others had no real affection for their birth parents but needed to know that they were safe and well. Some had a need to

rehearse first hand with their birth parents the story of their life while others wanted to obtain factual information.

(Macaskill, 2002, p 103)

Enabling attachment to new carers

Contact can enable attachment to new carers in a number of ways.

- Enabling the child to move on and attach to new parents with their birth parents' blessing, permission or approval.

- Promoting stability in a new placement by allowing the continuity of existing relationships to be maintained.

- Helping the child to understand the difficulties of their birth parents and avoiding idealisation, thus helping the child to understand past parental failings and why they needed an alternative permanent family.

- Reassuring the child about their birth relatives, including siblings, and allowing them to get on with life without unnecessary anxiety or distraction.

Achieving placement stability and security must be the prime consideration above all others, and if contact arrangements are serving to undermine that, then the other potential benefits will never outweigh the losses that this brings to the child. Early facilitative work with birth parents may help them to accept that they are not able to raise their child safely, and particularly after a permanence plan has been finalised, it is hoped that the parent would be able to put their own feelings aside and actively give their blessing to a child who is now living with another family. Working to achieve this is a delicate and challenging task for social workers who will need skills in managing defensiveness, resistance and shame.

Some parents can never accept the decision for a child to live permanently in another family, and if birth parents or others are actively determined to undermine a child's permanent placement, then this bodes badly for positive contact taking place. However, it is important to assess this carefully. The position of a parent who is fighting for their child in a contested court hearing should not be interpreted as the position that they may hold subsequently and into the future. In many cases, contact plans are first formulated in the context of such adversarial court cases and this makes the job of the assessing social worker particularly challenging.

For some children, thoughts and preoccupation with birth family can be all-encompassing and it is difficult for them to settle in their permanent home while they have unresolved feelings about birth parents or other family members. Children may feel guilty or disloyal for having abandoned their birth parents or birth family in favour of their new parents. In these situations, it may help children settle with their new family if they can maintain an existing relationship with family members, even if this needs to be limited in frequency and duration, and to be carefully supervised. Contact in this circumstance, particularly if children are prepared for it, can provide reassurance that their family is surviving and help children to experience the contrast of their lived experience in both families and avoiding the idealisation that can emerge after long periods without contact.

Promoting positive identity

Contact can play a part in promoting a positive identity through providing the child with genealogical and historical family information, specifically:

- allowing the child to get direct answers to factual questions about their early life or biological identity;

- providing information about family history and culture including birth relatives whom they resemble or from whom they had acquired special talents;

- allowing the child to develop an understanding of their ethnicity and culture, especially if their new family does not fully reflect their heritage;

- providing adopters and permanent foster carers with information and insight into birth family functioning and ethos, which in turn allows them to help the child to make sense of his or her history.

Children will have a developing identity that comprises aspects from their birth family as well as their new permanent family, and while permanence reports and life story books will often contain a lot of relevant information about a child's history with their birth family, it is inevitable that key information will not be recorded or will be lost. Family history tends to usually be passed on through an oral tradition, and children learn about themselves through stories retold and repeated in the family. Work in school about family trees or inherited medical conditions might generate questions about a child's own early life, or the lives of family members. Ongoing contact arrangements allow an opportunity for the child to explore their history and move towards a coherent narrative of the self.

Children in a new family of a different heritage may have particular interest in their birth family ethnicity and culture, which forms a central part of their identity. Some of these aspects can be observed if face-to-face contact is in place, and the cultural "difference" is experienced in the contact relationship with the birth family. Questions such as 'What were my first words?', 'When did I first walk?', 'Where was Granddad born and what did he do for work in his country of origin?' may emerge over time as the child becomes less preoccupied with loss or safety and more able to think and remember. Almost inevitably, a child placed with no contact will lose this detail forever, and contact can be a distinct benefit in enabling a child's access to historical, genealogical and very personal information – all of which is important in developing a sense of self.

Enabling emotional healing and promoting self-esteem

Children moving to new permanent families have usually been separated from their birth family because of neglect or abuse. They are likely to have experienced loss, trauma and feelings of rejection, and contact can play a part in emotional healing. It can:

- enable the child to achieve a realistic understanding of the circumstances surrounding their separation;

- allow the child to know that birth parents love him or her and are interested in their well-being;

- provide a degree of emotional healing when a birth relative is able to apologise to the child directly for abusive episodes;

- keep open the possibility of appropriate adult to adult relationships with birth family in the future;

- avoid a feeling of complete abandonment on the child's part – this can be experienced by some children as being worse than poor quality or limited contact.

Clearly, the extent to which birth parents or other family members can help a child make sense of their loss and trauma will depend on their insight and willingness to do this. Some parents will not be able to take responsibility for repairing the harm – they may not even be able to accept their part in it – and so will be unable to apologise to children. Others will be able to recognise that their problems have made them unsuitable parents and can let their children know this, and so absolve the child of the burden of guilt or self-blame. In some cases, parents will be able to put their abusive actions into context, for example, explaining to a child that they did assault them as a baby, but that they were young, depressed and experiencing domestic violence, and their loss of temper – although never acceptable – did not reflect a dislike of the child, but more an inability to cope.

For other parents, simply adhering to an agreed contact plan gives a message to the child that they love them and will never forget them. For a learning disabled parent it may be a message – even if not stated in words – which conveys that they love the child, they always have done, and they have always tried their best to care for that child, even if they were ultimately unsuccessful. In such circumstances, the child may only begin to understand what that means as they get older, but it might allow for some sort of meaningful relationship to develop. It may be that maintaining some contact throughout childhood makes it easier to establish an adult to adult relationship in the future.

The reality is that for many children, contact, where it happens, will be of a poor or limited quality. Parents who lose their children in a contested legal setting are by definition parents who have failed to provide for them, and usually have multiple problems. Nevertheless, for some children, the idea of complete abandonment by their parents – however ineffective they were in that role – can be devastating, and even very limited poor quality contact at least avoids that.

The challenge for the assessing social worker is to take all of the various factors into account, and arrive at a plan that best meets the child's needs in a challenging context. Part of that context must be the recognition that it is normal for an adopted or permanently fostered child to want information, and often to want contact, and that if the agreed arrangements do not provide this, then social networking activity might be seen as the alternative, with all the risks inherent in that.

The other key challenge is that of ensuring that children are provided with an honest and truthful account of their history, not a sanitised version that effectively leaves them confused (see Loxterkamp, 2009). Where children have been severely abused, there is no value in denying or minimising this, as this will not make sense when children ask 'Was it really necessary for me to be permanently removed from my family?' If direct contact is not deemed safe then children need to have a full understanding about why this is the case, and what might happen if birth family members find out where they are living. This is not about scaring children, but about ensuring they are realistic about their past, and helping them to consider the dangers of making contact through social networking.

Social workers who are developing contact plans need to start with an understanding of the purpose of that contact for the individual child. The form, frequency and duration of contact can only be considered when the purpose of the arrangements has been clearly identified.

3
Research evidence

INTRODUCTION

It is important that all social work practice is informed by research evidence, but the difficulty in relation to planning contact in permanence is that the research is both limited and inconclusive. The overall position, as described by Quinton *et al* in 1997, is little changed today:

> *In our present state of knowledge it is seriously misleading to think that what we know about contact is at a level of sophistication to allow us to make confident assertions about the benefits to be gained from it, regardless of family circumstances and relationships.*
>
> (Quinton *et al*, 1997, p 411)

> *Contact is a highly complex matter, especially difficult when the child continues to have a relationship with the birth parent guilty of abuse or neglect. And it must be appreciated that to arrive at balanced, well-considered decisions on contact in such cases makes near impossible demands on childcare professionals and substitute parents.*
>
> (Loxterkamp, 2009, p 424)

There have been no large-scale studies that compare outcomes for permanently placed children with and without contact, and finding sufficiently sophisticated methodology to reach reliable and valid conclusions in such a study would prove challenging if not impossible. Nevertheless, social workers are not operating in a research vacuum, and there is evidence about various aspects of contact with birth families that can inform practice.[3]

---

3   Research evidence in relation to contact in family and friends placements is considered in Chapter 7.

THE NEED FOR OPENNESS AND HONESTY

In counselling adults who were adopted as children in the UK before the 1970s, it became evident that the secrecy of the closed adoption model had left them with unresolved questions about their family histories, cultures and identities (Triseliotis *et al*, 1997; Howe and Feast, 2000). In more recent work, Morgan (2006) asked adopted children what they wanted to be told about their past and their responses confirmed the earlier research. Children wanted to know why they couldn't stay with their birth family; information about their birth family; information about their life before adoption; information about siblings; and whether they could make contact with their birth family. As a result of such evidence, the benefits to adopted people of having information about their origins is now widely accepted in adoption and social work practice, and information is provided in the form of life story books and later life letters. Neil *et al* (2011) note that where direct contact is working well it is significantly associated with higher levels of communicative openness amongst adoptive parents.

Preparation training aims to help potential substitute parents to understand that children – however young – will come to them with a past; and that, as their new parents, they will have a significant role in helping them make sense of and come to terms with that history. Part of any such preparation must be helping adopters and foster carers to understand how social networking can now be used to locate adopted and fostered children, and how these children can use this media to find their birth family. An absence of truth in telling children about the full extent of any abuse they have suffered and an absence of communicative openness make it more likely that children will resort to such approaches without involving a responsible adult.

FACE-TO-FACE CONTACT CAN WORK WELL

Grotevant *et al* (2004) provide compelling evidence from a longitudinal study to show that, for relinquished adopted infants in the US, ongoing face-to-face contact with birth families has worked very well. Those children as adolescents all, with the exception of one person, reported satisfaction with face-to-face contact arrangements and satisfaction was highest amongst those having the most contact. There was no evidence that openness had adversely impacted on the children's relationship with their adopters, or on their emotional and behavioural well-being. While clearly showing that direct contact in adoption can be hugely beneficial, it is important to recognise that this study was with relinquished infants, and cannot necessarily be transferred to older children or those who have suffered abuse and neglect in their birth families.

Neil's "Contact after Adoption" study (Neil 2004a; Young and Neil, 2009) considers a more typical group of adopted children in the UK context, including those who had been neglected and abused, having both direct and indirect contact. This study of children placed for adoption under four years of age included follow-up interviews with children, adopters and birth parents seven years after placement. The outcomes from this study in relation to direct contact are important:

> Face-to-face contact was, more often than not, very much liked by all parties. Most adopters and birth relatives got to know each other quite well and developed a trust in each other, enjoyed meetings and felt better informed about each other. Children generally did not show negative responses to contact meetings, possibly because in most cases they did not have an established relationship with birth relatives; contact meetings tended to be described as low key, like seeing a distant relative or friend of the family.

(Young and Neil, 2009, p 245)

An earlier longitudinal study by Fratter *et al* (1991) found that placement disruption in a large sample group of adopted and fostered children was less for those children who had face-to-face contact with a birth parent than for others. The study suggested that although face-to-face contact was not entirely without difficulties, for the most part it helped children and young people make sense of their histories, compared to those children without contact. Thoburn (2004) undertook a follow-up study and concluded that for the black and minority ethnic children, contact also played a part in contributing to a positive sense of ethnic and cultural identity.

Logan and Smith's study (2004, p 119) considered the cases of 96 children and young people in 61 adoptive families who were having direct post-adoption contact with both siblings and adult birth relatives, and overall concluded that 'the majority of direct contact arrangements were working well, several years after they had initially been agreed'.

Neil and Howe (2004, p 237) make the important point that 'young children (particularly those placed as babies) are currently the least likely to experience direct contact, at least in the UK context', and argue that the potential benefits that this could bring – primarily in relation to alleviating loss and promoting identity – are often overlooked. They argue that younger children are often better placed to have direct contact than older children as they have usually been less traumatised by the relationship with their birth parents, have less socio-emotional difficulties than children who are placed when older, and are more likely to be, or to become, securely attached to their new adoptive parents. The issue of age at placement is also noted by Biehal *et al* (2010, p 196) who state that children in permanent foster care appear more likely to be distressed by contact and more preoccupied with birth parents than those who were adopted, and who will usually have been separated from parents as infants.

While there is no suggestion that direct face-to-face contact is appropriate in all cases, research clearly shows that this form of contact can work well for many children who are adopted or in other permanent placements, and this will be particularly likely where:

- the child is placed at a young age, such as under two;
- the child is not exhibiting behavioural or emotional problems;
- the contact is with a relative who did not abuse the child;
- the adopters or foster carers practice communicative openness.

Given the challenges in preventing or limiting contact in an age of social networking (Fursland, 2010), it is all the more important for social workers to try and achieve direct contact where that is possible and in the child's best interests. If contact is denied or restricted, there is always the possibility that it might become established through social networking media, and this is likely to be unplanned, unmediated and potentially problematic.

FACE-TO-FACE CONTACT CAN ALSO BE PROBLEMATIC

Other studies have described more mixed outcomes, especially where children are older at the time of placement. Mackaskill (2002) explored the experiences of 106 children in 76 families who were placed at the age of four or over. The children were either adopted (about four-fifths) or permanently fostered (about one-fifth) and were having face-to-face contact with birth family members including siblings. Macaskill concluded that for an eighth of the sample the contact was positive in all respects, but for a quarter it was very negative, including children being rejected and emotionally harmed. For the majority (nearly two-thirds), the overall impact was categorised as either neutral or where 'positive aspects of contact were usually complexly interlinked with negative aspects' (2002, p 74). Sibling contact was slightly different in that this was a predominantly positive experience for the majority of children.

Macaskill (2002) also found that for some children, even where contact was felt to be broadly positive, it could provoke painful feelings that at times could be overwhelming. Some children were left feeling sad and disillusioned, and sometimes embittered by past memories. She suggests that at times contact plans (especially where contact was set at too high a level) could contribute to placements disrupting, but also concludes that birth parent refusal to have contact was often experienced as more devastating than living with the reality of an impoverished contact relationship.

Selwyn (2004) conducted a similar study of children who were placed at the age of three or over, who had plans for face-to-face contact with birth parents (31 per cent), other adult relatives (34 per cent) and siblings (90 per cent). This longitudinal study suggested that while most of the contact was still seen to be beneficial, particularly sibling and non-parent contact, there were negative aspects including abuse during unsupervised arrangements, and children showing significant behavioural difficulties before and after contact meetings.

Neil *et al* (2011) looked at direct contact arrangements in primarily adoption settings using questionnaires and interviews with social workers, adopters, and foster carers. This study reached similar conclusions to those noted above; in just under half of the cases, contact arrangements were working well, and in just over half there were "unresolved issues". Where things were going well, this was associated with children being aged less than two years at time of placement, the child not having emotional and behavioural problems, and where contact was with a person who had not abused them.

INDIRECT CONTACT CAN WORK WELL BUT CAN BE CHALLENGING

Neil's "Contact after Adoption" study looked at both direct and indirect contact arrangements and concluded that in terms of outcomes, 'the type of contact people were having (face-to-face or indirect) is less important than the quality of information exchange that takes place' (2004b, p 50). She suggests that indirect contact – the most common form for contact between young adopted children and their parents – can still allow for the communication of important information that can answer a child's questions, and can show that they have not been forgotten or rejected.

However, Neil goes on to suggest that there are many real obstacles with indirect contact that can adversely impact on the quality of information exchange. These obstacles can include difficulties within the agency acting as a third party such as delays, etc, but are mainly to do with the difficulty of communicating in writing where birth relatives and permanent carers may struggle to know exactly what to say; where correspondence crosses in the post so questions do not get answered; and where children, especially babies and toddlers, can be excluded from the process. Some adoptive parents do not like to write too fully as it might sound like they are boasting about their lives, and some birth relatives do not have the skills or confidence to convey what they really want to say, and may receive variable support from the agency. Furthermore, the very nature of indirect contact means that there is no immediate feedback, and no opportunity to observe reactions during communication.

In summary, Neil (2004b, p 63) concludes that 'indirect contact can be an effective means of all parties learning more about each other, but many hurdles have to be overcome for this to happen', and that 'indirect contact should not be considered an "easy" option'. For some children, indirect contact will likely meet their needs for information, but for others it will always be a second best to face-to-face contact.

NO CONTACT IS RIGHT FOR SOME CHILDREN

It is generally accepted, even by those who are strong advocates of the benefits of contact in permanent placements, that for some children it is entirely right that they do not have direct or indirect contact. Howe and Steele (2004) explain how, in certain circumstances, contact can be a hugely negative experience that can serve to undermine a child's relationship with a new permanent family:

> ...once a child has suffered from repeated incidents of trauma, relatively little is required on subsequent occasions...to trigger the same kind of responses that the initial trauma provoked...In effect, contact can re-traumatise the child. There is then the real danger that the child experiences the [new] placement as unable to offer a reliable or permanent sense of safety and security.

(Howe and Steele, 2004, p 213)

Contact that threatens placement stability is clearly not in the child's best interests and whether this takes the form of direct or indirect arrangements, would need to be stopped. For some children, having contact with people who abused them will not be appropriate, and can lead to further rejection and further emotional harm. Bond (2007) sets out the various circumstances when contact should not take place:

- when the child is at actual risk, or at risk of being re-traumatised;

- where the contact will leave the child feeling that that their new family is unable to protect them from danger;

- where the child is distressed to an extent that this outweighs any potential benefit from having contact.

Smith G (1995) considers situations where children's experiences of having been sexually abused means that a plan for no contact is appropriate. She notes that sexual abuse involves a distortion of relationships in a way that involves manipulation and coercive control that can continue even when the abuse has ended. Evidence about abusers teaches us that they can be extremely devious, and there are examples of the use of "hidden messages" in cards and letters that can serve to remind children of past abuse and past threats, re-traumatising children, further binding them to their abuser and preventing them from moving on.

> *In cases of sexual abuse, contact may impede the child's recovery by keeping the traumatic material alive. This needs to be said clearly and unequivocally.*

> (Smith G, 1995, p 88)

Both Bond (2007) and Smith G (1995) note the importance of listening to children and taking note of behavioural indicators that might suggest that no contact is a necessary plan. Loxterkamp (2009) takes the argument further and suggests that even where contact appears to be going well or well enough, it can be causing harm to the child. His key point is that where parents have demonstrated indifference or dislike towards a child, as they will have when they have abused or neglected them, to then try and give the child the message that they are valued and liked by the parents is problematic, paradoxical and difficult to achieve. It is suggested that in order to square this circle, professionals tend to offer children "sanitised" versions of their history, allowing for "ingratiating and falsifying communication" which does not actually help the child in making sense of their past. Loxterkamp (2009, p 435) concludes that 'contact can be a good thing only if the importance of truth is taken seriously and bad when truth is denied'.

THE IMPACT OF SOCIAL NETWORKING

Recent years have seen the growth of social networking and Simmonds, in the foreword to Fursland (2010), clearly sets out what this has meant in terms of adoption and contact:

> *...it is now clear that many people – adopted children and their adoptive parents, birth parents and other birth family members – and adoption agencies have been profoundly affected by the ease, directness and opportunities social networking sites make available. Social networking allows individuals to circumvent the agency's established role in preserving confidentiality, mediating information exchange and providing guidance and support. It has resulted in breaches of confidentiality and unexpected, unplanned and unthought-through contact resulting in distress, anxiety and unsettled young people and adoptive parents. It is a serious and worrying development. There are also examples where it*

*has provided opportunity for the exchange of information in constructive,
helpful and enriching ways.*

Fursland (2010) provides extensive case study evidence about the
negative impact of unplanned, unmediated contact on adopted children
and adoptive families, and the potential for such contact being initiated
cannot be ignored. When proposing plans for indirect contact or no
contact, social workers must be mindful of the possibility of unmediated
direct contact being established via a social networking site, and balance
this risk against the risks inherent in establishing a plan that involves
direct contact that might be mediated, restricted and managed. Where it
is simply too dangerous to allow any contact, it is important that children
and young people are engaged in work to help them understand the
reasons for this, and to help them to understand the risks inherent in
trying to trace relatives via a social networking site.

HOW MUCH CONTACT?

Although this guide focuses on planning contact, and does not consider
some of the more detailed practical discussion around implementing
and supporting contact, it is necessary to look at the question of contact
frequency, as in practice this needs to be considered at the planning
stage.

Mackaskill (2002) suggests that in relation to face-to-face contact with
adults, this needs to be at a frequency greater than once per year, as
annual contact does not allow sufficient continuity in the relationship,
and in terms of maximum contact levels suggests:

> *It is unlikely that a level of contact between children and their adult birth
> relatives that extends beyond four times annually will be manageable
> or practically viable in an adoption placement...[and] expectations that
> permanent foster carers could sustain levels of contact set as high as
> fortnightly or monthly were often totally unrealistic.*

(Mackaskill, 2002, p 54)

Smith and Logan (2004, p 183) similarly suggest that direct contact
of more than four to six times annually is likely to be problematic.
Mackaskill (2002) notes that contact with siblings could be sustained
at higher levels, reasonably being much more influenced by practical
considerations such as family lifestyle and geographical distance.

When planning frequency of contact, it is important to be mindful of the
age and stage of development of the child and their understanding of
"time". A child's concept of time can differ from that of an adult, with
time periods seeming collapsed or telescoped to children, so a level of

contact that is meaningful to adults may well be experienced differently and with some confusion by the child.

CONCLUSION

What all of this tells us is that contact planning is not an easy thing. Young and Neil (2009) sum up the position very helpfully:

Research undertaken in the last couple of decades has shown the potential benefits for all those involved that can be gained from contact. However, the research also highlights the risk of negative consequences which, in certain circumstances, may result. We are left with no simple answer to the question of whether contact will be beneficial within any specific adoption placement.

(Young and Neil, 2009, p 248)

Given the lack definitive messages for practice, Neil *et al* review the literature and offer a helpful conclusion:

It is clear from these and other studies that while contact can have beneficial effects, positive outcomes are not inevitable and the quality of contact must be considered.

(2011, p 29)

We cannot say that contact is good or bad in itself, or that direct contact is better or worse than indirect contact. We cannot conclude that more contact is better than less contact, or vice versa. It seems that what we can conclude is that children placed at a young age may more easily tolerate contact than those placed when they are older, and that whatever plans are put in place, the psychological openness of their primary carers will be of benefit to the child.

A good contact arrangement can take many forms, but must be rooted in a childcare plan that is based on a careful assessment of the specific factors in each case and the future needs of the child in terms of integration of their life history, curiosity about their past and the potential for repair in the future. Furthermore, the plan must be formulated with an understanding about social networking, about what this potentially offers to children who want to search for their birth family, and about the risks inherent in this approach. Practitioners will need to be mindful of the implications of this at the time of placement but also subsequently, and ensure that all parties are prepared for the possible scenarios that might follow.

4

The legal framework

ENGLAND AND WALES

Legal status and contact

The primary legislation which is relevant to contact in permanence (Children Act 1989, Adoption and Children Act 2002) applies in both England and Wales, as does the case law. However, the regulatory framework is different in each UK country, and so reference is made to both the English and Welsh regulations.

The legal framework for contact with children separated from their birth families varies depending on the legal status of the child and whether accommodation is provided to the child under the Children Act 1989 or the Adoption and Children Act 2002.

Where children are "looked after" by local authorities, they have a general duty under Schedule 2, paragraph 15 of the Children Act 1989 to promote contact between a child and his parents and other people connected with him, and paragraph 16 allows the local authority to make financial payments towards contact expenses in order to ensure that contact can take place.

Accommodated children

Where the parents have agreed to the accommodation of a child under s20 of the Children Act, they retain parental responsibility for the child and are able to make decisions about the child's contact with themselves, with family members and with any other person. Any contact order made under s8 of the Children Act will continue to be effective and must be implemented, and the local authority has no power to arrange or restrict contact other than in accordance with the parents' wishes. Arrangements for contact must be included in the child's care plan and placement plan and must be subject to consultation with the parents, child and any other relevant person (s22(4) Children Act, Regs 4, 5 and 9, Care Planning, Placement and Case Review (England)

Regulations 2010) and Regs 4, 5 and 7, Placement of Children (Wales) Regulations 2007).

Children in care

Where a child is subject to a care order or interim care order under s31 or s38 of the Children Act, the local authority has a duty under s34 to allow reasonable contact between the child and his parents, guardian or special guardian, any person who has parental responsibility for him and any person who had a residence order or High Court order giving him care of the child. Any of these people, any other person who gets leave from the court, the local authority and the child may make an application to the court under s34 for a defined contact order and the local authority may apply under s34(4) for authority to refuse contact between the child and any person who would otherwise be entitled to reasonable contact. The local authority may also refuse contact for up to seven days in an emergency (s34(6)).

Reg. 8 of the Care Planning, Placement and Case Review (England) Regulations 2010 and Regs. 2 and 4, Contact with Children Regulations 1991 (Wales) set out the notification requirements with which they must comply when such a decision is made. A s34 contact order may also be varied by agreement and on written notice as set out in Reg.8(4), Care Planning, Placement and Case Review (England) Regulations 2010 and Reg. 3, Contact with Children Regulations 1991 (Wales).

Children placed for adoption

If a local authority is authorised to place a child for adoption, either by consent under s19 of the Adoption and Children Act 2002 or by a placement order, or if a child under six weeks old is placed for adoption, all provision for contact under the Children Act ceases to have effect. The local authority will no longer have a duty to allow contact under s34 and any contact order made under s34 or s8 will no longer have any effect.

No further application for a contact order under the Children Act may be made, but the court may make an order for contact under s26 of the Adoption and Children Act, either at the same time as making a placement order, or on application by a person who would have been able to apply for an s34 order or who is a relative of the child. S27 allows a local authority to suspend any contact for seven days in an emergency and allows an application to be made to vary or revoke the s26 order.

Once a child has been placed for adoption, the Care Planning, Placement and Case Review (England) Regulations 2010 (Reg.3) and Reg.3(3) Placement of Children (Wales) Regulations 2007 no longer apply. Where a child is placed for adoption, parental responsibility will be shared between the local authority, the prospective adopters and the birth parents. The local authority will decide the extent to which each exercises their parental responsibility, but usually decisions on contact will be made by the local authority, not by the prospective adopters.

Adopted children

The making of an adoption order brings to an end any order, including contact orders, made under the Children Act. Once a child has been adopted, the birth parents have no parental responsibility for the child and have no legal connection with the child which would give them the right to apply for a contact order under s8 of the Children Act, though they may make an application for a s8 order to be heard at the same time as an adoption order. S1(6) requires the court to consider all the powers available under the Adoption and Children Act and under the Children Act before coming to a decision about a child's future, and s46(6) requires the court to consider the arrangements for contact before making an adoption order.

Case law on adoption and contact

Contact orders attached to adoption orders are rare. In *Re R* [(adoption: contact) [2005] EWCA Civ 1128,] Wall LJ reviewed earlier authorities and stated 'that the imposition on prospective adopters of a contact order which they are not in agreement with remains extremely unusual'. This was quoted with approval in *Oxfordshire County Council v X, Y & J* [2010] EWCA 581 Civ; adopters' successful appeal against an order requiring them to provide photographs of the child to the birth parents.

It is important that contact issues be taken into account at the matching stage (Adoption Agencies Regulations 2005 Regs. 31(2)(c) and 32(3)(b) (England) and Regs. 32(3)(b) and 33(3)(ii) Adoption Agencies (Wales) Regulations 2005), rather than attempts being made to impose contact plans on reluctant adopters subsequently. Contact should usually be the subject of agreement at the time of the adoption order, but where adopters have agreed to a contact arrangement, and subsequently have a change of mind, this could give a birth relative grounds to be granted leave to make an application for a contact order. This was the situation in *Re T* (Minors) (Adopted Children: Contact) [1996] Fam 34 where a girl was given leave to apply for contact where adopters had failed, without giving any reason, to provide an annual report on her adopted sister.

Children subject to special guardianship orders

Where a child is placed under a special guardianship order, the parents will retain parental responsibility but the carers will acquire overriding parental responsibility for the child. Before making a special guardianship order, the court is required, by s14B(1), to consider whether a contact order should be made and whether any existing s8 order should be varied or discharged. Without an order, contact arrangements will be a matter to be negotiated between the parents and carers wherever possible.

The parents will have the right to apply for contact with the child under s8 of the Children Act and the court will consider the case on its facts, having regard to the welfare checklist in s1, and there is no legal presumption about the level of contact that would be appropriate where the child is expected to remain permanently in such a placement.

The court will be able to order support for contact arrangements by making a s11A contact activity direction if appropriate, and support for contact arrangements may also be given by a local authority as part of a special guardianship support plan.

Children subject to residence orders

Where a residence order has been granted in respect of a child, the carer will share parental responsibility with the child's parents, and contact will be a matter to be agreed between them. In default of agreement, the parents, carer or the child may apply for an s8 contact order. The court may also make a contact order at the same time as a residence order even though no application has been made, applying the welfare checklist in s1.

NORTHERN IRELAND

Legal status and contact

The legal framework for contact with children separated from their birth families varies depending on the legal status of the child and whether accommodation is provided to the child under the Children (Northern Ireland) Order 1995 or placed for adoption under the Adoption (Northern Ireland) Order 1987. Issues around contact are also addressed in the Contact with Children Regulations (Northern Ireland) 1996.

Where children are "looked after" by the Health and Social Care Trust (HSCT) – whether they have been voluntarily placed in care or were made subject of care orders – HSCTs have a general duty under Article 29 of The Children (Northern Ireland) Order 1995 to promote contact between a looked after child and his parents and other people connected with him, and Article 30 allows the HSCT to make financial payments towards contact expenses in order to ensure that contact can take place.

Accommodated children

Where the parents have agreed to the accommodation of a child under Article 21 of the Children (NI) Order 1995, they retain parental responsibility for the child and are able to make decisions about the child's contact with themselves, with family members and with any other person. Any contact order made under Article 8 of the Children Order will continue to be effective and must be implemented. The HSCT has no power to arrange or restrict contact other than in accordance with the parents' wishes. Arrangements for contact must be included in the child's care plan and placement plan and must be subject to consultation with the parents, child and any other relevant person.

Children in care

Where a child is subject to a care order or interim care order under Article 50 or 57of the Children (Northern Ireland) Order 1995, the HSCT has a duty under Article 29 to allow and promote reasonable contact between the child and his parents, or guardian, or any person who has parental responsibility for him and any person who had a residence order or High Court order giving him care of the child. Any of these people, any other person who gets leave from the court, the HSCT and the child may make an application to the court under Article 53 for a defined contact order and the local authority may apply under Article 53(6) for authority to refuse contact between the child and any person who would otherwise be entitled to reasonable contact. The HSCT may also refuse contact for up to seven days in an emergency. An order made under Article 53 may be varied or discharged by the court, and Regulation 3 of the Contact with Children Regulations outlines the actions which an HSCT is required to take before it can depart from the terms of a court order on contact.

Children placed for adoption

A child may be placed for adoption pursuant to the agreement to adoption of each parent or guardian or by virtue of a freeing order under Article 17 or 18 of the Adoption (Northern Ireland) Order 1987. While a freeing order discharges a care order with the associated contact requirements, the court can decide to make an Article 8 contact order at the same time as making a freeing order.

In practice, however, the courts in Northern Ireland have tended to take the view that when making a freeing order, it is preferable to allow the HSCT flexibility in relation to contact arrangements, and there have therefore been few contact orders made alongside freeing orders. It could be argued that relatively high levels of direct contact, comparative to other jurisdictions, have continued to prevent Article 8 orders being imposed/sought, not fully recognising the post-freeing context as significantly different from the pre-freeing context where HSCTs are required to promote contact.

Adopted children

Article 12(b) of the Adoption (Northern Ireland) Order1987 provides for the court to impose such terms or conditions as the court thinks fit when making an adoption order. The courts have generally taken the attitude there is no need for a contact condition to be imposed if agreement can be reached between the adoptive parents and those seeking contact, but can, in exceptional circumstances, impose a contact condition against the wishes of the adoptive parents. Even though this provision is rarely used, it could be suggested that the possible threat of its imposition has resulted in higher levels of contact than in some other UK jurisdictions.

Unless an applicant can apply as of right for a contact order under Article 10 of the Children (Northern Ireland) Order1995, an applicant who wishes to seek contact after an adoption order has been made must seek the leave of the court to make an application for a contact order.

Case law

It should be noted that the case law discussed above in relation to England and Wales is pertinent to Northern Ireland, as legal precedents here often emanate from English cases.

Children subject to residence orders

Where a residence order has been granted in respect of a child, the carer will share parental responsibility with the child's parents, and contact will be a matter to be agreed between them. In default of agreement, the parents, carer or the child may apply for a contact order under article 8 of the Children (Northern Ireland) Order 1995. The court may also make a contact order at the same time as a residence order even though no application has been made, applying the welfare checklist.

SCOTLAND

Introduction and welfare and other principles

When decisions are made about contact in Scotland, the most important principle is that the child's welfare is the decision maker's paramount consideration. This has been embedded in Scots Law since the Law

Reform (Parent and Child) (Scotland) Act 1986. Section 3 of that Act required this in private law cases about children: custody (now residence), access (now contact) and a range of related matters.

The Children (Scotland) Act 1995 extended this principle from private law cases to courts and hearings in children's hearing cases; to local authorities for looked after children; and to courts in parental responsibilities orders and adoption applications. The principle, along with others, has been repeated in the Adoption and Children (Scotland) Act 2007, and also in the Children's Hearings (Scotland) Act 2011. The Adoption Policy Review Group Report (2005) was very clear that contact for children must be based on their needs and welfare; and this has been reiterated in court judgements such as *East Lothian Council, Petrs.* [2012] CSIH 3, an appeal court decision in an application for a permanence order with authority for adoption.

As well as the "welfare" principle, those making decisions about contact have to take account of the views of children and young people; the "minimum necessary intervention" rule; and children's religious persuasion and racial origin and cultural and linguistic heritage. Under the 1995, 2007 and 2011 Acts, these principles must be used in all proceedings about children and their situations, except in the children's hearing system.

One of the difficulties for courts and hearings is to distinguish the different purpose of contact in permanence cases from the intentions when children are likely to return home or there are good bonds which need to be maintained where families have split up and private law arrangements are being considered. It is helpful to bear this in mind when planning contact in permanence cases and to consider addressing the different purpose in reports.

Legal status and contact

The legal framework for contact with a child separated from the birth family varies depending on the child's own legal status.

Where a child is looked after by a local authority, the authority have general duties under s17 of the 1995 Act. These include duties to promote regular contact between the child and people with parental responsibilities, as appears 'both practicable and appropriate' to the authority, bearing in mind their duty to promote the child's welfare, s17(1)(c). This means that the duty to arrange contact is not absolute but is subject to the "welfare" duty.

Every looked after child must have a child's plan, in terms of Reg.5 and Schedule 2 of the Looked After Children (Scotland) Regulations 2009 as amended. Arrangements for contact between the child and his or her family must be included in the child's plan. The child's case and plan, including the contact arrangements, must be reviewed regularly, even if the accommodation is provided for respite or is otherwise short-term.

Children subject to residence orders

When contact arrangements and decisions are being made in court cases involving individual parents and/or other people with an interest in the child, s11 of the 1995 Act applies. Section 11(7)(a) says that the court must regard the child's welfare as paramount when making any order under s11, including contact ones. The other principles also apply.

When a residence order is granted for a child to live with a relative or kinship or foster carer, the order gives the carer(s) the parental right to control residence and other responsibilities and rights in ss1 and 2 of the 1995 Act. Apart from the right to control residence, these responsibilities and rights will be shared with the parent(s), depending on what the individual order sets out. If contact arrangements can be agreed, the court will not make a contact order, because it is not necessary. If arrangements cannot be agreed, and the court thinks that contact is in the child's best interest, the s11 order will provide for contact. However, the court will avoid making prescriptive arrangements unless this is absolutely necessary. If contact is not appropriate, the order may state that there will be none.

Whether or not there is a contact provision in the s11 order, anyone with an interest, including the child if he or she is old enough, may apply to the court to vary the arrangements.

Children accommodated under s25

Where the parents have agreed that their child should be looked after and accommodated under s25 of the 1995 Act, the parents retain all parental responsibilities and rights and there is no statutory order. The parents may therefore make decisions about contact for and with the child. If the local authority feel that such contact is harmful for the child, they should consider what other steps they need to take to protect the child, including statutory ones.

Children looked after and placed through the hearing system

Where a child is subject to a supervision requirement away from home, under s70 of the 1995 Act, contact between the child and parent(s) is decided by the children's hearing. Contact will usually be a condition of the supervision requirement, which sets out details of the arrangements.

A supervision requirement, including contact, is reviewed by the hearing from time to time, and every case must be reviewed at least once a year.

Parents and other relevant persons, and the older child, may call a review any time three months after the previous one. The local authority may ask for a review at any time. A review hearing will look at all aspects of the requirement, including contact.

If someone has a contact order under s11 of the 1995 Act, that cannot be enforced while the child is subject to a supervision requirement and the hearing will make all the decisions about contact. A supervision requirement may therefore make contact arrangements that are contrary to those in the s11 order, and these take precedence over the s11 order.

Under the 2011 Act, supervision requirements are re-named compulsory supervision orders (CSOs) and interim ones are also possible. However, the arrangements for contact in CSOs and interim CSOs are similar and contact directions may be part of them, in terms of s83(2)(g).

Children looked after on permanence orders

Every child subject to a permanence order is a looked after child, whether the order includes authority for adoption or not, s17(6) of the 1995 Act. A permanence order may be a "destination" order, to secure long-term arrangements short of adoption, such as permanent fostering, or it may be a route to adoption.

When the court is deciding any permanence order application, contact is one of the matters it will consider. The report for the court from the local authority must include the proposed arrangements for contact if and when the order is made, and this applies to all applications, with or without authority for adoption. The relevant court rules are r.31(2)(b)(viii) of the Sheriff Court Adoption Rules 2009 and r.67.28(2)(b)(viii) of the Rules of the Court of Session. The court will consider contact against the background of the long-term plans for the child and as part of the child's welfare and the other principles (or conditions) in s84 of the 2007 Act.

The appeal court stated in an application for a permanence order with authority for adoption, *East Lothian Council, Petrs.* [2012] CSIH 3, that the issue in deciding about contact is 'whether or not ongoing contact would safeguard and promote [the child's] welfare'. The test was not met just because there was no evidence of harm to a child in continuing with contact; and the fact that a parent wants contact to carry on is not of itself a reason for not granting a permanence order.

When a permanence order is made, the ancillary provisions may include contact arrangements for the child with parents and anyone else where that is appropriate, whether the contact is direct or indirect. If contact arrangements are agreed and working well, there may be no need for contact ancillary provisions. On the other hand, the court may include ancillary provisions about contact, although it will always prefer these to be as general as possible, rather than setting out prescriptive arrangements.

As a result of the complicated provisions in the 2007 Act, the court has to make sure that the parental right to contact remains with some person. This means that where contact is not appropriate, there may be an ancillary provision which restricts contact to nil but does not remove a parent's right to contact.

When a permanence order is made, it revokes previous orders under s11 of the 1995 Act (s88 of the 2007 Act). This means that any existing contact order will be wiped out. In addition, when there is a permanence order for a child, no one may apply for a s11 contact or residence order, s11A of the 1995 Act, inserted by s103 of the 2007 Act.

If changes are wanted to contact provisions in a permanence order, any person with an interest may apply to have the order varied or revoked. However, everyone apart from the local authority which holds the order must seek the leave of the court to go ahead with a full application, ss92(2) and (3), 94(4)–(6) and 98 of the 2007 Act.

Children placed for adoption

A child is placed for adoption by an adoption agency under the Adoption Agencies (Scotland) Regulations 2009. Placement for adoption occurs when that agency has made decisions that adoption is the best plan for a child and to "match" the child with specific approved adopters, Regs.13(1) and 8(1) respectively. The decisions are made after the agency's adoption panel has made recommendations about these matters.

Where a child is simply placed for adoption under the 2009 Regulations and is not also looked after by the local authority under a statutory order, arrangements for contact, if any, have to be agreed between the birth parent, the adopters and the adoption agency. The birth parent(s) retain full parental responsibilities and rights until an adoption order is granted. Neither the adopters nor the agency have these and contact therefore has to be what, if anything, the birth parent(s) wish. In practice, placements under the 2009 Regulations, without any order, are almost always where the parent(s) fully agree with the child's adoption, such as when a child is relinquished.

Most children who are placed for adoption under the 2009 Regulations are also subject to a statutory order, either a supervision requirement or a permanence order, with or without authority for adoption. The prospective adopters are usually also approved foster or kinship carers. Any contact will be regulated by the child's order, as outlined above. If the child is subject to a supervision requirement, the parents retain parental responsibilities and rights, but the arrangements for contact are decided by the hearing. If the child is subject to a permanence order, the local authority will have some parental responsibilities and rights, and may have almost all of them. Ancillary provisions will usually set out what contact, if any, the birth parent(s) have. If there is no ancillary provision about contact, it would normally be up to the local authority to decide what contact there should be.

Adopted children

When a court is considering an adoption application, contact is one of the matters it can look at. This is true whether the child has been placed for adoption by an agency, or in all other types of cases. There is no explicit statutory requirement on the court specifically to consider post-adoption contact, unlike that in s46(6) of the Adoption and Children Act 2002. Where the adoption follows a permanence order with authority for adoption, the birth parents may receive a copy of the adoption application, especially if there was an ancillary provision about contact. This does not give them back their rights to consent or not consent to adoption, but they may come to court to seek continuing contact or to make new arrangements.

The court will consider contact against the background of the planned adoption and as part of the child's welfare and the other principles (or conditions) in s14 of the 2007 Act. The most important one is to treat the child's welfare throughout life as its paramount concern, and this obviously includes future arrangements such as for contact. The comments about contact in *East Lothian Council, Petrs.* [2012] CSIH 3, a permanence order application mentioned above, are equally applicable in an adoption case.

When making its decision, the court has two reports in every case, as well as evidence, particularly in disputed cases. These reports should cover all aspects of the child's welfare and the proposed adoption, and can and should raise any issues about and plans for post-adoption contact, direct or indirect. The reports are prepared by the adoption agency or local authority and the curator, and there are detailed court rules about the contents in the Sheriff Court Adoption Rules 2009 and the Rules of the Court of Session.

When an adoption order is made, it removes all parental responsibilities and rights from the birth parents, and from a local authority and anyone else having them under a permanence order, which ceases to have effect, s102 of the 2007 Act. Responsibilities and rights are transferred to the adopters, and they have the right to make or refuse any arrangements for contact in the future.

A condition about contact may be attached to an adoption order, s28(3) of the 2007 Act, but this is rarely done in practice. In *B, Petr*, 1996 SLT 1370, decided under the Adoption (Scotland) Act 1978 Act, the appeal court held that a condition should only be attached to an adoption order in "exceptional circumstances". Normally, the court leaves contact matters on a voluntary basis, trusting the adopters to act appropriately for the child's welfare.

If the child was subject to a supervision requirement, it is normally terminated by the court which grants the adoption, although it may continue. If it is not terminated, the adopters are relevant persons and the birth parents have no further rights to attend hearings or seek contact.

If adopters do not keep to informal arrangements about contact, or the birth parents otherwise want to seek post-adoption contact, they may apply for this under s11 of the 1995 Act. However, if the adoption was granted under the 2007 Act, they will require the leave of the court to go ahead with a full application.

5
Assessment

INTRODUCTION

> *Decisions about contact must...be made in relation to the needs, characteristics and circumstances of particular children and their families rather than in response to general evidential rules or ideological commitment.*

> (Smith and Logan, 2004, p 35)

Having identified the purpose of contact and recognised the potential benefits of contact in permanence, each case will need to be assessed individually in order to see what benefits, if any, can *actually* be achieved. This will entail looking at any contact that is already in place, and considering the characteristics of the child, the birth relatives, and – if they are identified – the adopter or permanent carer.

From the outset, the assessor must be clear with all parties that contact plans will be determined by what is in the best interests of the child or children. This could include aspects that indirectly benefit the child, for example, arrangements that leave the primary carer feeling supported and confident. Contact plans should never be used as a bargaining tool within legal proceedings, or as a "reward" to adults for taking a particular course of action.

THE CHILD

Wishes and feelings

The child's wishes and feelings about proposed contact plans need to be ascertained and taken into account, having regard for their age and understanding, and recognising the complex feelings that might be involved.

Children's feelings about contact were related in complex ways to how they made sense of their parent's past and recent actions, their age at entry to care and, to some extent, their carer's attitude to contact.

(Biehal *et al*, 2010, p 196)

It is therefore not simply that practitioners should ask the child exactly what they want and then aim to deliver this. Things are more complicated than that and, as Macaskill (2002) and others point out, children often want more contact than they can emotionally manage.

...we find ourselves in a position where we may have to listen to the children's wishes and feelings and filter them through our understanding of their desperate desire for the love of an abusing parent and concern for their well-being.

(Lindsey, 2006, p 225)

What children want and what children need may be different things. While children's views must be taken into account, it is their best interests that are paramount. But this is not straightforward. Even where practitioners are of the view that contact might not be desirable, it may still be best to allow it:

...when children are determined that they need to see their birth family, despite professionals' conviction that it is not to their benefit, refusal may result in the breakdown of the placement. It may be preferable for the child to experience the distress and disappointment that may arise from their unfulfilled hopes for the contact experience but make the decision themselves. The capacity to hold the child through this experience is crucial.

(Lindsey, 2006, pp 228–9)

Other children are not enthusiastic about contact, and 'unhappy memories of abuse, neglect or rejection could make them feel angry or ambivalent towards birth families' (Biehal *et al*, 2010, p 194). It is for the assessing social worker to engage with the child and help them to think about all aspects of their relationship with their birth family. This will mean making sense of the past, reflecting on the present, and beginning to think about how this relationship will change when they are permanently cared for outside of this family.

Equally, it will be important to consider the child's perspective even where they are non-verbal due to either age or impairment. This might involve the use of specific communication techniques with disabled children, and/or a greater reliance on observation and interpretation of what is observed. Kenrick describes contact between Joe and his birth mother, involving Joe's carer Paula:

After two months of three-times-weekly contact at approximately the age of five-and-a-half months, Joe began to become much more distressed during the contact visits. Paula could hear him getting more worked up and crying in quite a different way to any that she had ever heard, different in quality. Increasingly his distress could be seen to start as she left the room. She saw birth mother trying to comfort Joe by jiggling him, she thought much too vigorously, and being unsuccessful. It became the practice, after ten minutes of inconsolable crying, that she would return to the contact room and comfort Joe until he was more relaxed. Then she would leave the room again. When Joe again became more distressed she would have to return. She described her anguish while listening to him crying, wanting to be with him to help him and knowing that she could not go until the agreed time.

(Kenrick, 2009, p 9)

Although Joe is too young to be asked about his views on contact, it is probably fair to say that at this time he is not enjoying the experience, and it is not meeting his developmental needs. Other babies and some profoundly disabled children might convey their pleasure from contact meetings through smiles, facial expressions and noises, and a good assessment will reflect this. Where a child is saying that they do not want to have contact, or it appears to be re-traumatising them, this should be viewed very seriously; contact in such circumstances can leave the child feeling that their new carers are unable to keep them safe.

Existing contact

The child's expressed wishes and feelings will need to be considered alongside observations of any existing contact arrangements, to contextualise whatever they are saying. If the child is describing a close emotional connection with their mother, but observations suggest that the mother is uninterested and preoccupied during contact meetings, then this will need further exploration. If the child says they want very regular sibling contact but observations indicate that time together is used by one child to bully and demean the other, this will not be straightforward. Equally, the child might feel angry at their parent for their failings, and say they want no contact, but an objective assessor might nevertheless identify much about the contact meeting that is positive.

A good assessment will need to consider the child's behaviour before, during and after the contact meeting, taking into account the views of the child's current carers who are often best placed to understand some of this. Assessors will need to be careful not to over-react to normal upset or over-excitement that is displayed by children in what is an emotionally charged setting (Triseliotis, 2010), but must at the same time take this into account.

Attachment history

It will also be necessary to reach a view about the quality of the child's relationship with his or her birth parents or other relatives, taking account of the child's history, developmental functioning, resilience and attachment patterns. It is the child's attachment to significant adults that will best inform contact planning; a child who has experienced good pre-placement care (often by someone other than their birth parents) will generally be well placed to achieve and sustain a secure attachment to new carers while at the same time managing contact with birth family. These children are likely to make good socio-emotional progress. Children who have experienced poor care from depressed, ambivalent or abusing parents will often bring with them dysfunctional and disorganised patterns of attachment that require careful observation and interpretation.

Siblings

An assessment will also need to be made of a child's relationship with his or her siblings, whether they are adopted or fostered separately, or living with birth family. From a child's perspective, sibling relationships will be important insofar as they will have a shared history, but siblings will also be the relatives who usually know the child for the largest part of their life. In planning sibling contact, it will be important to involve the carers of those siblings, and consider issues of openness as well as being clear about the purpose of the contact. For some siblings, decisions will have been made that they cannot permanently live together, but nevertheless can gain much from ongoing contact.

Other significant people

It is important to remember that different cultural groups apply different meanings to particular kin relationships and it may be that within some communities the family group is viewed more widely than just being the nuclear family. This may mean that cousins, aunts and uncles or family friends from the same locality are seen as important members of a child's network.

In cases where the child has not had a close relationship with a particular relative (as is quite often the case with babies and infants), that relative may nonetheless be able to offer information, support and affection during childhood or into adulthood, and the potential benefits for the child in the short and long term should not be overlooked. Grandparents may be particularly well placed to fulfil this role. Again, the assessor will need to be clear about the purpose of any proposed contact in terms of how it meets the developmental needs of the child.

For some children maintaining their relationship with foster carers is important, and any assessment will need to think about whether this is desirable, taking into account the child's views and wishes alongside other factors. If they are old enough, it is important to get a sense from the child of who is important to them and why.

Summary

There are a number of questions that need to be considered in relation to the child and ongoing contact.

- Who are the people who are most important to the child; who do they have existing relationships with?

- What, if any, are their expressed wishes and feelings, and have all efforts been made to elicit these?

- What is the observed quality of the child's relationships with birth parents and other family members?

- What does the child's developmental and attachment history tell us?

- What behaviour is seen before, during and after contact and what is the significance of that behaviour?

- Are there people who can play a positive part in the child's future although they currently have a limited relationship with the child?

THE BIRTH FAMILY

Wishes and feelings

Contact arrangements need to be considered in relation to the benefits that they will bring to the child, but should also be informed by the wishes and feelings of the birth parents or other relevant adults. The assessor will need to find out what they expect to achieve from contact, whether they have any insight into how contact might meet the child's needs, and how they feel about the fact that the child will be moving to another permanent family. Do they understand that within adoption the child will likely take another name, and how do they feel about that? Have they thought about their child calling other people "Mummy" or "Daddy" and considered how the child will likely come to see their new family as more relevant to them than their old one? If they cannot accept this, contact might prove challenging, as they will need to behave in a way that does not leave the child with divided loyalties.

Ideally, the parent or adult will accept that a court has decided that permanence outside of the birth family is in the child's best interests, and try to do their best for the child in this new context. In cases where the parent is able to acknowledge and apologise to the child for past abuse or failings, and/or give their blessing to the new arrangement, this can have significant developmental benefits. It also bodes well for high quality and meaningful contact, with the potential for a more positive relationship with both the child and their permanent carers to develop over time.

However, this is a lot to ask, and the majority of birth parents will not be in favour of the adoption or other permanent arrangement. While there is no evidence that this is a contra-indicator to successful contact, if any face-to-face contact is going to be viable birth parents will need to recognise that their child will not be well served by attempts to challenge or undermine the new arrangement. While they are entitled to maintain a view that the separation was wrong, they must be able to manage their feelings and behaviour in a way that contributes to the child settling and moving forward in their new family, even if they understandably would have preferred the situation to be different.

In deciding what contact plan might work best, it is important to recognise that how parents feel during an adversarial court case might not always be a good indicator of their longer term views; and in some cases birth family members may come to see that adoption or permanent fostering was in fact right for their child. The requirement for a contact plan to be presented as part of a permanence plan within the court arena does bring potential difficulties, and this work will need to be undertaken sensitively and carefully. Lindsey writes:

> At the point when decisions are made in the courts about contact, the birth parent may frequently not yet have had the chance to do the mourning work and come to terms with the loss of their child...It is therefore important to acknowledge the process that has to take place for birth families and to recognise that their capacity for contact may change and may respond to sensitive therapeutic work.

(2006, p 230)

When the local authority is progressing a plan for a child to be permanently cared for outside of their birth family, this is always going to make working relationships with parents challenging, and in some cases it may be that the work in relation to contact is best undertaken by someone other than the child's social worker.

It is also helpful if birth relatives can understand that they are not being guaranteed a regular, fixed contact arrangement, but that contact will change as dictated by the child's ever-changing needs. If contact is presented as an "entitlement" or an incentive to encourage birth relatives to accept a plan for adoption, it does not assist them in accepting the reality of adoption as being for the child, and can set them up to feel betrayed when contact needs to change from what they feel they were promised.

History of abuse

In considering the potential for contact, it will be necessary to think about any abuse or neglect that the adult might have been responsible for. Some children come from backgrounds where they have suffered horrific cruelty that amounts to torture and in such cases contact is unlikely to be appropriate. Others will have experienced sexual abuse within a dysfunctional extended family network, and may suffer from severe emotional trauma if contact is permitted, or even if the whereabouts of their new carers is known (Smith G, 1995). In such cases, it might well prove difficult to monitor or supervise indirect contact in the form of letters or cards, as these could include coded messages that only make sense to those who had been involved in the abuse.

In other cases, birth parents may have decided, entirely reasonably, that it is best to relinquish a baby for adoption, but want to agree an appropriate contact plan. Learning disabled parents may simply lack the ability and/or support required to adequately care for a child, but nevertheless have done their best to care for them, and wish to remain a part of their lives as much as is permitted. For others, poor mental health, drug and alcohol misuse, sometimes combined with social factors such as poverty and domestic violence, mean that children have been neglected or come to other harm.

> It was easier for children to make sense of the fact they were no longer with their birth parents if they understood this as being due to parents' inability to care for them, due to their learning disabilities or mental health or substance misuse problems.

(Biehal *et al*, 2010, p 193–4)

In these cases, there may have been positive elements to the parenting that was provided, and the fact that ultimately the parents were deemed unable to care for the child does not mean that there cannot be benefits from some continued contact. Assessing workers need to be clear about how contact might best achieve these benefits, and this will be particularly challenging if an adult's ability to meet the child's needs varies from day to day.

Relationship with the child

The quality of the attachment, and the capacity of the parent to nurture, will be important considerations in planning contact. Research evidence in a child protection context (Smith *et al*, 1995) has revealed that "low warmth-high criticism" parenting styles are particularly damaging to children; and there may be situations where the adult's capacity to respond appropriately to the child is so limited that contact is not viable. In other cases, birth parents may be skilled at communicating warmly with their children, notwithstanding other problematic aspects that prevent them from parenting, and it may be that some face-to-face contact in such cases will bring huge benefits to the child.

Ability to adhere to plans

Contact is likely to be difficult and painful for birth relatives, sometimes so much so that they cannot bear to keep in touch, or if they do this is intermittent, irregular or unreliable. For others, it is their own difficulties or lifestyles which mean they are unable to prioritise the needs of the child. Birth parents have almost by definition huge vulnerabilities such as mental ill health; drug and alcohol dependence; learning disabilities; difficulties managing anger and aggression and, crucially, in accepting support. These factors can often mitigate against them fulfilling contact agreements.

Whatever the reason, inability to adhere to contact plans is likely to reawaken feelings of insecurity and loss in the child, risking distress if they have built themselves up to attending contact and are excited, but then are let down by the other party not attending. This raises difficult questions which need to be considered on a case-by-case basis about whether it is preferable to make plans that avoid this scenario or support the child to make sense of it.

It will also be important to talk with parents about social networking, and wherever possible achieve an understanding about why attempting to trace or contact children through this medium is unhelpful and unacceptable. A genuine commitment to avoid this, and to respond appropriately if they are approached by the child, would bode well in terms of an assessment about the extent to which these birth family members might be able to adhere to agreed plans.

Risk assessment

Any assessment of contact with the birth family will need to incorporate a risk assessment, considering risk to the child and their new family in terms of both physical and emotional harm. This could be a particularly significant issue in deciding whether face-to-face contact might be appropriate, or whether any exchange of information will need to be via a third party. In looking at these issues, the assessor will also need to take account of the potential for contact to be initiated through social networking sites, and to ensure that the plan has measures in place to manage this if necessary.

In large part, the risk assessment will be informed by behaviour to date. At the most extreme end, where birth relatives have attacked or threatened foster carers or others, and/or have long histories of violent behaviour in other settings, it is likely that direct contact will not be viable, even if there is no perceived risk of violence to the child. Where birth parents have made every effort to comply with agreed plans and expressed their differences calmly and appropriately, then the opposite will be true.

In many cases, the reality falls somewhere in between and the assessment will need to look at the details of the case to decide the level of risk that any particular arrangement brings, and how this compares with any alternative contact plan. Such an assessment needs to be undertaken with care to avoid unhelpful generalisations. It is probably understandable for a parent to express anger towards the social worker taking their child, but this should not in itself be a reason to conclude that they will always behave angrily in other settings.

In cases where an adult has been deemed a significant risk and denied contact, it will be necessary to consider the issue of maintaining confidentiality if consideration is being given to direct contact with other relatives or friends. In situations where a mother has an "on-off" relationship with a father who has been denied contact, then it would be very risky to arrange for that mother to have direct contact, even if she appeared to be separated at the time contact was being planned. Similarly, making arrangements for grandparents to have direct contact might require confidence that they are able to put the needs of their grandchild before the wishes of their own children for information about addresses and the like.

In making any plans, assessing social workers need to work on the understanding that it is not possible to keep identifying information confidential where there is face-to-face contact. Children will talk about themselves and their lives and cannot be coming to contact scared of divulging anything about their home life. It is easy to imagine a four-year-old who is proud to recount their name, address, school and teacher, as this is often what they will do in other settings with adults. It is crucial to feel confident that birth relatives having face-to-face contact do not present any risk to the new permanent carers, and would not try to seek out their child. This is especially important with the advent of social networking and the ease of tracing that the internet now offers once a surname is known.

Grandparents and other adult relatives

Birth family grandparents in particular can be important people for an adopted or permanently fostered child, and are often well placed to offer the various benefits associated with contact. In many cases they will not have had the troubled relationship with the child that the birth parents had, or the strong feelings about their own failings, and so can be very well placed to promote and encourage attachment with new families. They will usually be well placed to share genealogical and historical information, and where they have a mature and balanced approach, might be able to help the child understand that he or she is not to blame for the failings of their birth parents. All of these aspects will need to be considered within the assessment.

Siblings

Sibling contact can potentially offer a number of benefits to children who are permanently living apart from each other, not least because it can lead to a lifelong relationship with people who, by definition, have much in common. Such contact can provide opportunities to make sense of the past as well as providing ongoing genealogical information, and reassurance that each party is well and thriving. Research and anecdotal evidence suggests that children can often accept and benefit from more frequent contact with siblings than would be appropriate with their birth parents or other adults.

However, for some siblings decisions will have been made to deliberately place them apart, and these cases in particular demand very careful assessment. There is the danger of negative patterns being repeated if one sibling had seriously dominated or bullied the other, or where two or more children were involved in inappropriate sexual behaviour. There may also be intense rivalry and aggression that adults struggle to manage, and this clearly would make face-to-face contact a challenge.

Confidentiality is also an issue where one child has links such as direct contact with a birth parent while the other doesn't.

Summary

There are a number of questions that need to be considered in relation to the birth family and ongoing contact.

- What are their expressed wishes and feelings about contact and do they recognise the needs of the child?

- What is the observed quality of relationships with the child, and do they convey warmth and affection?

- Do they accept the new carers as the child's primary family, and if they are ambivalent about this, can they nevertheless behave appropriately with the child?

- Is it likely that the birth family member will adhere to the agreed contact plan?

- What role did the birth family member play, if any, in abuse or neglect of the child, and how do they view that now?

- If the person was not the abuser, do they understand the harm that was done, and the risk the abuser posed or poses to the child?

- If they are being considered for direct contact, will they be able to maintain appropriate confidentiality (including from other family members)?

- Has a risk assessment been undertaken?

- Can the birth family member play a positive part in the child's future and, if so, how?

THE ADOPTERS OR PERMANENT FOSTER CARERS

In the majority of cases, a contact plan is required at a relatively early stage, where court proceedings are ongoing, and before adopters or permanent foster carers have been identified. In these cases, the social worker will need to assess the child and their birth family, and often formulate a contact plan without reference to the potential permanent carers. Although this practice guide specifically relates to the making of the contact plan before permanent carers have been identified, it is nevertheless worth making some comments about this third part of the adoption triad.

All prospective adopters and permanent foster carers should have been prepared and assessed in relation to their understanding of the continuity needs of children whom they hope to care for, including the possibility of contact emerging via social networking. As a minimum, it should be expected that they understand that an openness of attitude will serve them and their child best whatever the contact arrangements, but ideally they should be committed to fulfilling the assessed needs of the child for direct or indirect contact and be open to the possibility that these plans might change in the years ahead. By the time of approval, it should be clear about their individual preferences or strengths in relation to different contact arrangements and how this might work in practice, and this ought to be a significant factor within the matching process.

However, where an adopter or permanent carer is already identified, including where the child is already placed with them, the assessor will need to involve these carers in the assessment process.[4] This can have

---

[4]   This is often true for kinship carers. See chapter 7 for more discussion of the specific issues on those cases.

potential benefits. Lowe *et al* (1999) found that adoptive parents were not always as willing to adhere to contact plans as would have been hoped, and so involving them in the initial discussions and decisions would make it more likely that they will have a better understanding of the purpose and benefit to their child, and therefore a commitment to implementation.

In making contact arrangements with identified carers, their understanding and ability to think reflectively about the benefits and challenges of contact will need to form a part of that assessment. There is a pressure on potential substitute parents before the placement has been agreed and it is important that the assessor is clear that any agreement that is made is not on the basis of feeling they have to "jump through hoops" or feeling coerced. It will be necessary to explore their perception of the child's wishes and feelings, and their psychological openness to discussing the child's complex feelings and memories that will be stimulated by contact. The assessor will need to know whether the carers are emotionally robust, and whether they feel confident in their relationship with the child. It will also be necessary to see whether they have empathy for the birth family, and to convey an honest but respectful attitude towards them, whilst demonstrating a flexible and collaborative approach to making contact work. All of these factors would bode well for successful contact.

Contact is known to work well where the permanent carers feel that they are in control, and therefore have the confidence and insight to share that control with birth relatives. This is most likely to happen and to work well where birth relatives accept the authority of the adopters as the day-to-day parents of the child, and where the adoption agency provides good quality support to all parties.

In some cases, proposed substitute carers will be opposed to contact. It is hoped that in such circumstances the social worker would discuss the benefits of contact, understanding that most adopters and foster carers want what is best for their child. Continued resistance to contact after such discussions would create a real dilemma, and ultimately a decision would have to be made about whether the proposed carers are well placed to meet the child's needs, and whether disrupting a stable placement overrides the benefits of achieving contact in another placement. Such cases are complex, and an assessment will need to take into account a variety of factors.

Summary

There are a number of questions to be considered in relation to the assessment of adopters or foster carers and their role in contact planning for children.

- What are their expressed wishes and feelings about contact and do these recognise the benefits to the child?

- Do they show an openness of attitude and what are their views on direct and/or indirect contact arrangements?

- Do they understand the implications of social networking and what that might mean in their particular situation?

- Are they confident in themselves and in their relationship with the child?

- Can they empathise with the birth family and convey information about them positively but honestly to the child?

6
Myths and misunderstandings

There are a number of commonly held myths or misunderstandings that can unhelpfully interfere with good quality contact planning. This chapter sets out these myths and offers a response to each of them.

Contact is disruptive to placements and stops children from attaching to their new family

Loxterkamp argues that later-adopted children will inevitably have longings to be with their birth family, and 'these longings will interfere with the forming of secure relationships with the adoptive parents and family' (2009, p 425). However, the majority of studies (even those with later-adopted children) conclude that the evidence does not support this claim and, to the contrary, suggest that an appropriate contact plan can have developmental benefits for the child that in turn will help them feel settled and attached to their new family (Bond, 2007, p 1). As more is understood about attachment theory and the biological, psychological and social effects of good care, the old-fashioned, but sometimes still mentioned idea that children cannot manage multiple attachments has now clearly been disproved. Wisdom from multi-generational extended families where child rearing is a shared activity lends weight to the idea that children can transfer attachments. The challenge is often about helping children to re-work their attachment strategy. There will be circumstances where contact does undermine attachment, but that will be in relation to the specific circumstances of the case, and cannot be generalised.

Even if the child can manage such contact, it will serve to undermine the permanent carers and this will adversely impact on the child

In reviewing the literature, Smith and Logan conclude that 'post-adoption contact does not seem to interfere with adoptive parents' sense of security or their sense of "entitlement" to their children and may actually enhance these feelings'(2004, p 35). The fact is that if children are having their developmental needs met, they are likely to be happier and more settled. This in turn will make it easier for adopters and permanent carers to feel positive and confident about their role. While there may be specific cases where existing permanent carers are feeling undermined by contact arrangements, this is likely to be the result of specific characteristics of either the permanent carers or the birth family or both, or as a result of inadequate or rushed assessments where parties were not actively engaged at an early stage.

Direct contact with a birth parent (or other adult family member) is not appropriate if he or she does not agree with the plan for permanence

Contact plans are often being formulated while court proceedings are ongoing, and birth parents or other family members may be fighting to have their children returned to their care. Sometimes they are unrealistic about their ability to parent, and often they are angry about their children being removed, but there is no evidence to suggest that this means they will be unable to subsequently participate in a positive direct contact arrangement. If they were not fighting for their child, this would likely be interpreted as them not being interested or caring enough, and so parents find themselves in a double-bind. Practitioners need to be sensitive to this.

That is not to say that parental attitudes about any subsequent permanent placement are irrelevant however, and careful discussions are needed at an early stage to consider how they might be able to participate in contact if adoption or permanence was to become the plan. In the context of an adversarial court battle this will probably not be an easy conversation, but one that is necessary in order to meaningfully assess the contact options. It must be remembered that positions can and do change, and a parent saying that they will never give up on their child is very different from them saying that they will attempt to undermine any future placement.

If there is evidence that children are unsettled before or after contact, then contact is not working and should be stopped

While there will always be a few children for whom contact is simply too disruptive or upsetting, for the majority there will be benefits alongside more challenging aspects. As Triseliotis points out:

> As contact is such an emotive experience for both parent and child, it has to be expected that for a period of time afterwards the child may still be reacting to the engagement, irrespective of whether it was positive or negative...children usually look forward to contact, commonly want more contact than they get, but are nevertheless commonly upset by it.

(2010, p 63)

Birth parents might find themselves in a double-bind here. If the child is visibly upset following contact then this is viewed as problematic, but if they are not, it is viewed as the child considering the contact as unimportant and therefore of little value. Neither interpretation is appropriate. Bond suggests that 'in relation to all aspects of contact, it is generally better to help children manage the pain they experience, rather than try to cover it over' (2007, p 44). Careful engagement with the child about their experience is needed and ideally this should be a shared responsibility between the carer and the social worker, and should include an exploration of the issues with birth parents.

Where a child does not have a strong attachment then contact, especially face-to-face contact, is not important

Contact can serve a number of developmental purposes for children, and maintaining an existing relationship is only one aspect. Even for children who are neutral about contact, there will likely be benefits to them in terms of providing historical and genealogical information and helping them to better understand their families of origin. Furthermore, research suggests that it is the children who are least embroiled in the family history and dynamics, usually those placed for adoption at a young age, who are least emotionally stressed by contact, including face-to-face contact, and so best placed to manage this without disruption. Although the research is not conclusive on this point, there are also indications that for some children and birth families, indirect contact can be less effective than face-to-face contact as a medium for information exchange.

The child does not talk to their adopters or foster carers about their birth family and this means they do not matter to them and contact is unnecessary

Cleaver found that 'it was rare for children to make their views on contact known to either carers or social workers' (2000, p 272), but that does not mean that contact in these cases serves no useful purpose or that children do not have a view on it. The fact that a child does not talk about their birth family can be interpreted in a number of ways. Maybe the contact arrangements are working well and meeting the child's needs in relation to this aspect of their life so they do not feel the need to discuss matters much in between contact meetings. This may change as the child matures and becomes more curious about his or her history. Or maybe they are reluctant to mention birth family because of the reaction they expect or have experienced from adopters or foster carers, either overt or covert.

Face-to-face contact is most appropriate for older children; babies and infants don't need this as they have no existing meaningful relationship

Ironically, and somewhat counter-intuitively, research tells us that children placed as babies and infants are often emotionally more able to manage contact than older children (Neil and Howe, 2004). Babies and infants will have spent less time with birth family, may have experienced less extensive developmental harm, and will usually be better settled and integrated with their new families. They will often not have explicit memories of abuse and neglect, making contact meetings less emotionally charged. However, the adult network should be vigilant for any changes in behaviour or ability to settle in even the youngest child. Older children, by contrast, may want high levels of contact but will struggle to manage this, as they find themselves with all sorts of confusing feelings, including possibly divided loyalties. They may or may not want to sustain the relationship and might not be able to appreciate that contact serves a number of purposes and maintaining an existing relationship is only one of them.

Indirect (letterbox) contact is easier to manage than face-to-face contact

From the perspective of agencies, it is often felt that letterbox contact is easier to manage than the demands of face-to-face contact, but research (Neil, 2004b) would suggest that this is not the case. Although indirect arrangements *can* be effective, communicating through the written word can be challenging, in terms of avoiding misunderstandings, conveying exactly what is intended, and getting the right tone so that letters are not seen as cold and uninformative. For indirect arrangements to work well it is suggested that both parents and adopters will need support and mediation, and this is particularly true of birth parents who may have poor literacy skills or whose first language is not English, or whose language does not translate to the written word. Furthermore, the growth of social networking (Fursland, 2010) means that the old certainties about being able to block any attempts at direct contact no longer apply.

Where cases are complex, indirect contact once or twice a year should be the "default" position

Indirect contact is not always as straightforward as it seems, and it offers a very different experience to direct contact. Direct face-to-face contact, when it works well, allows children to "see for themselves", offers better opportunities for the parties to build empathy and understanding with each other, and adds to a bank of shared memories for children and relatives. However, when it does not work well or is inappropriate, there may be very good reasons to avoid such direct interaction. The point is that it is unhelpful to have any default position; rather, it is necessary to identify the purpose of contact, and then look at how best to set up arrangements to achieve that purpose.

Where contact is included in the child's plan, especially direct contact with birth parents, this will put off potential adopters

There is anecdotal evidence of adoption social workers advising children's social workers to avoid having a plan that involves direct contact as this makes recruiting adopters for them more difficult. This may or may not be true, but contact planning needs to be based around meeting the needs of the child, not around the needs of adopters or adoption agencies. If prospective adopters do not understand why contact is important, then this is something that needs to be better addressed in their assessment, preparation and training. If children's identity needs and other developmental needs are being met through appropriate contact plans, then this will also benefit adopters who ultimately will want what is best for their child.

Social networking presents significant challenges to contact planning; but since we can't control this it is best to ignore it

It is true that social networking has made it extremely difficult to keep control of contact plans, particularly where children want to find their birth family. It is also true that "the genie is out of the bottle" and we cannot go back to the way things were before social networking websites existed. However, this does not mean that we should ignore the issues. On the contrary, social workers need to make sure that they fully understand the implications of social networking for contact, so that planning takes full account of the possibilities that might develop, and also so that they can ensure adopters and foster carers fully understand the issues. More than ever, this development highlights the importance of working openly and honestly with children so that they are involved in formulating, and fully understand the reasons for their contact plans.

Once a contact plan has been agreed then this should be implemented until the child reaches adulthood

While it is important that all parties enter into an agreed contact arrangement in good faith and with a commitment to adhere to the plan, it is equally important to recognise that things might change – especially for the child – and that any contact plan must be subject to review and revision according to circumstances. Birth relatives need to understand that the contact plan agreed at the outset is the plan that appears appropriate at that time, but it is not possible to predict the future, and they have no "entitlement" to contact if it is not meeting the needs of the child. This could mean a decrease in contact, or an increase, or a change in the structure of that contact, depending on the individual circumstances of the case. Adopters and permanent carers will be key people in identifying where contact needs to change, and they will need good quality support in considering and implementing any such changes.

7

Contact in kinship care

INTRODUCTION

Kinship care, in the context of this chapter, refers to permanent substitute carers who may also be known as family and friends carers or connected persons.[5] In practice, these carers will often be grandparents, aunts, uncles or siblings, but also might be cousins or other blood relatives. Some kinship carers will be friends of the child or their family, or exceptionally will have a professional connection to the child, for example, being the child's school teacher or youth worker.

In many ways, the issues discussed elsewhere in this practice guide – including the importance of communicative openness – apply equally with family and friends carers as they do with other substitute carers. However, the situation is complicated by the fact that kinship carers are already identified, are usually already caring for the child, and often have an established relationship with the birth parents, for better or for worse. What this means is that it is necessary to consider contact arrangements in an already established framework of relationships, and in a context where children have often been abused or neglected by family members, with the added dynamic that this brings.

RESEARCH

Hunt *et al* (2010) summarise the literature on contact in kinship arrangements and conclude that, on balance, kinship arrangements tend to result in more frequent and consistent contact than when children are living with "stranger" foster carers.

This study looked at 113 children of various ages and ethnicities in kinship foster placements who were subject to care proceedings during

---

5   In this chapter kinship or family and friends carers refers to adopters, special guardians, foster carers, holders of a residence order, or private foster carers, unless specifically stated.

the latter half of the 1990s. Just under two-thirds were living with grandparents and about one-quarter with aunts or uncles. The original plans for 86 per cent of children included face-to-face contact with at least one parent, and for half of this number it was with both parents. Of the remainder, nine per cent had no contact and four per cent had indirect contact plans. Three years after the proceedings, 83 per cent of mothers and 59 per cent of fathers who originally had a plan for face-to-face contact were still participating, although frequency of contact levels had reduced.

About one-third of the sample experienced the contact as either positive or not detrimental, leaving two-thirds where there were either negative aspects to the contact (42 per cent) or the contact was predominantly negative (21 per cent). The study revealed that relationships between carers and parents, although mixed, were seriously strained or conflicted in about 20 per cent of cases.

Farmer and Moyers' (2008) study compared a total of 142 kinship placements with 128 stranger foster care placements. In relation to contact, the study revealed that children in kinship placements had higher levels of contact with aunts, uncles and cousins than children in stranger placements, and where they were placed with paternal family members, also had more contact with fathers. However, difficulties in the relationships with family members emerged for over half of the family and friends carers compared with only 16 per cent of unrelated carers:

> Some parents were resentful that a relative had taken over the care of their children. Other parents were actively hostile to the kin carers and a few made threats or actually attacked them, while others made false allegations against the carers or undermined the placement in other ways.

(Farmer, 2009, pp 20–21)

Wellard (2011) similarly indicates that for the grandparents in her small-scale study, relationships with the children's mothers were a source of ongoing difficulty and stress in most cases, sometimes requiring non-molestation orders or injunctions to be taken out. Fathers in this study were predominantly entirely absent or having very infrequent contact, and the grandparents talked about trying to help the children cope with the disappointment when contact plans were not adhered to, or parents showed no interest in them.

Aldgate's (2009) study of 30 children in kinship care in Scotland suggests that contact with birth parents was not entirely satisfactory. Although 22 of the children had contact with their mothers, and 16 children had contact with their fathers, the vast majority said that they wanted more contact. Where children had no contact with their birth parents, they tended to say that they were content with this, but the researcher notes that it was hard to know whether this was their genuine view or whether they had been influenced by their carers. This study found few children who had all their siblings living with them, but most of them did have contact with siblings.

The research also gives rise to concerns about the quality of contact assessment and planning (as well as management):

> The only time when contact with parents was terminated was as the result of advice from psychiatrists or other specialists. In many other cases more active management of the contact by social workers was needed so that children did not receive confusing messages from parents about their ability to care for them and so that placements were not undermined. It is important that consideration is given to limiting or terminating contact when it is clearly detrimental to children.
>
> (Farmer, 2009, p 21)

Hunt *et al* (2010, p 84) also conclude that efforts by social workers to predict where contact might be problematic were not very accurate, and parental attitudes to the placement at the outset were not a good indicator of subsequent outcomes. Farmer (2009) adds that social workers were less likely to supervise kinship contact than contact involving children placed with unrelated carers.

IMPLICATIONS

What emerges from this brief review of research is a picture whereby contact levels with birth family are usually higher than in stranger permanent arrangements, and more likely to include face-to-face contact. However, as with stranger carers, while some contact arrangements serve children well, contact is not always experienced as positive.

The research also reveals high levels of stress for the carer in managing contact, and suggests the need for better support for kinship carers in this area.

There is little evidence of effective practice in these studies, and it may be that social workers were tending to assume that contact would take place and it would run smoothly, simply because the child was living with relatives. However, the additional complexity that comes from a placement where birth parents often have an established relationship with the child's carers makes a good quality in-depth assessment all the more necessary.[6]

STATUTORY GUIDANCE IN ENGLAND

In response to such research findings, Statutory Guidance on family and friends care in England states that:

> ...management of contact can often be a source of considerable anxiety and conflict for family and friends carers. It can place emotional and practical strains on all the parties involved. Family dynamics and relationships may be fundamentally changed, particularly for grandparents and others who are becoming "second time round" carers...Information should be made available to family and friends carers about local contact centres and family mediation services, and how to make use of their services.

(Department for Education, 2011, p 25)

The same guidance is also clear about the role of the local authority in promoting and supporting safe contact where this is in the interests of the child:

> Where there are safeguarding concerns there may be a need for the involvement of children's care services to support safe contact arrangements. Contact may be limited through a court order...[and may] need to be carefully managed, monitored and supported, to ensure that it does not become unsettling and possibly harmful for the child. Local policies should identify services available to family and friends carers to support the management of contact arrangements, and where necessary to offer independent supervision of contact.

(p 26)

While there is no equivalent guidance in Scotland, Wales or Northern Ireland, best practice demands that these aspects are considered and addressed in those countries.

---

6   The impact of difficult family dynamics could not have been more clearly illustrated than in *Re L* (Special Guardianship: Surname) [2007] EWCA Civ196 [207] 2 FLR 50; a case where maternal grandparents holding a Special Guardianship Order in respect of their grandchild, wanted greater authority in being able to determine contact with their daughter and the child's father. Primarily as a result of the problematic family relationships evident in this case, Right Honourable Lord Justice Ward decided that a contact order was necessary, and that contact needed to be supervised by the local authority away from the grandparents' home. He added that the money expended on the legal process might have been better used to fund family therapy.

ASSESSING CONTACT IN KINSHIP CARE

The same issues that need to be considered for children who are adopted or permanently fostered outside the family equally need to be considered for those who are permanently cared for by relatives, but the assessor will need to be sensitive to the existing relationships between all three parties in the arrangement.

While some family and friends carers are well placed to decide upon and manage contact with birth parents and other family members, the research findings set out above show that for many this is not the case. Any assessment in relation to family and friends will need to look at the following issues, in addition to the issues that are relevant to non-related adopters or foster carers.

- If the child is already placed, how has contact been going to date, and what role has the carer played in this?

- Is contact working well for the child and for all other parties, or does it need to be revised?

- How does the carer feel about birth parents and others having contact, and how is this conveyed to the child?

- Does the carer fully understand any risk to the child from birth parents or others, and are they able to protect the child from such risk?

- How well does the carer demonstrate communicative openness in relation to the child's relationship with birth parents and others?

- What is the relationship between the carers and birth parents (or others having contact), and how has this been historically?

- If contact must be limited, then how will this impact on the relationship between the carer and the other family member involved?

- Does contact create stress or conflict, and how is this managed? How has conflict been managed or resolved in the past?

- Would mediation be useful and if so does the local authority have a role in helping to set this up?

- What role might any third party usefully play in facilitating contact arrangements?

- What support might the local authority need to provide to make contact work better?

- Does the local authority need to take responsibility for supervising the contact?

Central to any contact plan must be the safety and best interests of the child, and just because their placement is with a family or friend does not change this fact. Although there are specific issues to consider from the perspective of the carer in these cases, this should not mean that the assessing worker loses focus on the child and their developmental needs.

At the same time, the assessing worker will need to be mindful of how contact, if not appropriately set up and supported, has the potential to undermine a family and friends placement. It is likely that contact in such cases will be more frequent than in adoptive placements, and has the potential to be more informally arranged and supervised. The carer will need to feel confident about any plans that are in place, and must have an opportunity to receive support if they feel this is needed. The nature of supervision will need to be carefully considered in order to maximise the opportunities for children's continuity needs to be met.

In the same way that communicative openness underpins any effective contact plan for unrelated carers, so it does when carers are family or friends. This will involve providing a context that allows for reflective communication about the circumstances that brought about the placement, the role of birth parents and other family members in the child's life now, and what meaning the child ascribes to these people and events. It will also mean reflection about the future, and some thinking about how relationships will develop over time. These conversations may not be easy – either for the child or for the carer – but establishing a family culture in which this dialogue can take place will undoubtedly be in the child's best interest.

In practice, many family and friends carers might struggle to offer this communicative openness; as well as being carers, they are also part of a family network and might have understandably strong views about the behaviour of their adult children or siblings whose child they are caring for. To step back and offer a reflective and therapeutically positive interaction with children might be too much to ask without effective and intensive support, particularly if carers continue to be perceived negatively by that birth parent, remain subject to criticism or verbal abuse, or have been seriously wronged in the past.

Barratt and Granville give the example of how this can be particularly difficult for sibling carers.

> Sibling carers may have suffered themselves at the hands of their own parent, and there may be rage at the absent or failed parent on their own as well as their sibling's behalf...While anger at the parent can be energising, it may also make it harder to see a younger sibling's different feelings or experiences... This can leave both carer and child with unhelpful, stuck stories about the history.

(2006, p 172)

In Roth *et al* (2011), sibling carers recounted the difficulties of being in conflict with their parents over contact. At times they had to stand up to the wishes and demands of parents who felt themselves to be in a position of parental authority over the sibling carers themselves, as well as the children they were raising.

With family and friends carers, it will be for the assessor to explore such issues, reach a judgement about the impact of the carer's position in the context of the child's holistic needs, and to formulate a workable contact plan that takes this into account. Sometimes it will be about getting a balance between what is desirable, and what is achievable. Sometimes it might be about trying to compensate for the carers' limitations through other resources. In any event, this will need to be a key part of the assessment, and brings at least as many challenges as formulating a contact plan with permanent carers who have no existing relation with the child or his or her family.

8
Conclusion

THE CONTEXT

Attitudes over the years to openness in permanence have been largely influenced by the social context in which social work operates, but also increasingly as the result of the emerging research. This has clearly shown that the perceived benefits of secrecy and a "clean break" do not serve children well now – if ever they did – and that whatever contact is envisaged, the child will get most from this in a context where their primary carers can demonstrate communicative openness in all respects.

Although it is not as sophisticated as we would like, there is now a body of research evidence to assist practitioners in making contact plans. This tells us that dogmatic or doctrinaire approaches that either champion or reject contact are not helpful, but that instead situations need to be carefully assessed on an individual basis, taking into account a variety of factors. We know that for some children, contact, including face-to-face contact, will serve them well (particularly when they are placed for permanence at an early age); for others, including older children, the findings are more mixed, but there are arguments for helping older children to manage the difficulties rather than trying to avoid them. For some children, any contact with certain individuals will not be in their best interests, and all arrangements will need to be reviewed and revised on an ongoing basis.

THE PURPOSE OF CONTACT

To make an appropriate contact plan, it is important to be clear about the purpose of contact, with absolute clarity that any arrangements are designed to benefit the child in the short and longer term. Inevitably, in some situations this will not meet the needs of the adults involved. Practitioners must understand that contact, whatever form it takes, has no inherent value unless it meets a developmental purpose such as:

- enabling attachment to new carers (by countering feelings of guilt, anxiety and self-blame, and by avoiding idealisation);

- promoting positive identity (by providing the child with genealogical and historical information);

- enabling emotional healing and promoting self-esteem (by dealing with loss, trauma and rejection).

Some children will benefit in all these respects; others only in some. For some children, their developmental needs will actually be best met by denying contact; instead assisting the child's understanding of their separation in the context of a communicatively open relationship with their primary carers, and ensuring a continuity of narrative for the child. Even where there is no contact, the child must never be expected to sever relationships with his or her family of origin, who can never be erased from his or her memory. There is no such thing as a "fresh start".

ASSESSMENT

The challenge for social workers is to identify when contact is in a child's best interests and what form, if any, it should take. This requires an in-depth, high quality assessment looking at the child, the birth family, and the adopters or permanent carers if they have been identified. It also needs to consider issues of attachment, the impact of abuse and neglect, and family dynamics.

While the interplay of various factors will need careful consideration, and every case must be assessed on its individual merits and in the context of what can realistically be achieved, there are certain factors that might make contact more likely to achieve positive outcomes:

- where the child is resilient, emotionally and behaviourally stable, and has a strong sense of permanence (often associated with being placed at a young age);

- where the child desires contact and does not appear to have an adverse emotional or behavioural reaction to it;

- where the contact is with a family member who did not directly abuse or neglect the child;

- where the child understands that his or her parent or family member is unable to care for them due to factors such as ill health, learning disability, or substance misuse;

- where the parent or family member accepts their own past failings and gives the child permission to settle with their new family;

- where the parent or family member shows a commitment to contact, and demonstrates a warm child-centred approach;

- where the carer (if identified) is confident and positive about the contact plan.

Similarly, there are factors that indicate contact might have less successful outcomes:

- where the child is opposed to the proposed contact;

- where the child's behaviour significantly deteriorates either side of contact and these difficulties endure for an extended period;

- where the child has been sexually abused involving manipulation and threats;

- where the birth parent or family member remains adversarial and committed to undermining the new placement;

- where the birth parent is critical of the child and struggles to show warmth or understanding;

- where contact puts either the child or the new family at real or perceived risk;

- where the new permanent family (if identified) believes that contact will threaten the stability of the placement.

Where all the factors identified as likely to achieve a positive outcome exist in a particular case, it would be fair to suggest that relatively high levels of face-to-face contact might be appropriate. Where all the factors indicating less successful outcomes exist, then it is probable that no contact is the most appropriate plan. Where there are both positive and negative features, it will be necessary to look at how to achieve the best outcome and to minimise the risks involved. This will include making decisions about whether face-to-face or other direct contact is most appropriate, or whether indirect contact can achieve the same purpose. It will also involve thinking about how contact might develop through social networking sites, and ensuring that plans are in place to try and avoid this and manage it if prevention is not possible.

Making judgements about contact is not easy, nor is it something that can be achieved as a "one-off" piece of work. Instead, judgements will flow out of an established and effective working relationship with all the parties in the permanence triad (the child, the birth parents/relatives and the substitute carers, where identified). It is crucial that the contact assessment is undertaken by a well informed practitioner; there are numerous myths and misunderstandings about contact, and these must be disregarded where they have no evidential base.

In the age of social networking, the possibility of children tracing birth relatives or being traced by them cannot be ignored, and the best defence against this is direct work with children about their life story and identity. As Loxterkamp (2009) makes clear, children and young people need to know the truth about the past, not a sanitised version, both in order to reach a coherent understanding of their situation, but also so that they can better understand the potential consequences of making contact through a social networking site or through other means.

KINSHIP CARE

Research suggests that the most challenging contact arrangements are those proposed with birth parents who have severely abused their children, and at times social workers might conclude that contact in such circumstances is undesirable. However, in these cases there may be other family members, such as siblings, grandparents, aunts and uncles, who can play a significant role through contact with the child. It is important that social workers consider these family members carefully, and as individuals, looking at how they could contribute in a child-centred way.

This is also true in relation to assessing for contact where children are living with kinship carers, circumstances that bring into play additional challenging factors. In these circumstances, the child's carer will not only know the birth family, but will usually be a part of it, holding views, opinions and feelings borne out of a shared history, and may be drawn into a coalition against the local authority. All of these complexities will need to be taken on board, with recognition that while much practice will apply equally to stranger carers and kinship carers, the latter will also have specific needs arising from the uniqueness of their situation.

THE CHALLENGE

Planning contact is not easy, but neither can it be ignored. There are numerous children who have benefited from carefully considered and well thought out contact plans, and numerous others who feel they have missed out on a shared history, a sense of identity and relationships with siblings and extended family members. This can leave them feeling "incomplete", sometimes into old age. Social workers, with the support of others, shoulder a huge responsibility in trying to get this right.

Appendix – Case studies

CASE STUDY: WILL, CHRIS AND NEIL

Chris, Neil and Will are white British children, brothers aged three, four and five. Their mother, Pamela, has a mild learning disability and spent a childhood in care characterised by a number of placement moves and abuse by various carers. Steven, the father, also has a learning disability, combined with depression, and struggles with anger management.

Until two years ago, the family all lived together with Steven's parents. During this period there were various concerns about the children being neglected, inadequately supervised and witnessing parental disputes that fell just short of domestic abuse. After a number of referrals to children's services, a conference was held and it was decided that the children were in need of a protection plan. Despite high levels of support, matters did not improve, and the older boys' behaviour was becoming of increasing concern.

Police were called to the home late one evening to find various adults arguing and shouting, and the children running around unsupervised in the garden. As a result of this incident, the children were accommodated, and care proceedings were initiated. The family attended for a residential assessment where it became clear that the children were not getting the supervision, stimulation or emotional warmth that they needed, and Steven was handling them roughly when managing their behaviour. After an incident where the parents were arguing and Will was pushed out of the way, the assessment concluded early, offering evidence that the parenting of the boys was not good enough. The assessment also suggested that Will's behaviour was most concerning, and that this included some quite serious bullying of his younger siblings.

Foster placements were arranged with Chris and Neil living together and Will being placed in a different foster home close by. Chris and Neil thrived in foster care and a number of their problematic behaviours disappeared, although it was of concern that Neil demonstrated sexualised behaviour in his play and made concerning comments of a sexualised nature. Will settled less well, continued to demonstrate extremely poor relationships with children and adults, and disclosed serious sexual abuse by a range of adults including both parents. He said that Neil had experienced this also, but that Chris had not been involved. Over a period of time Neil made similar disclosures, consistent with the information that Will had given, and it became clear that the boys had been forced to undertake sexual acts with each other.

It was decided that Chris and Neil should be adopted together, and that Will would need further therapeutic work before considering whether adoption might be possible for him. This plan was backed by the Guardian and a number of experts.

The parents, through their solicitor, opposed the adoption, but also argued strongly that if it went ahead they wanted direct contact with the boys. When this was rejected, the parents requested indirect contact in the form of sending cards and gifts for birthdays and Christmas, arguing also that they had a right to know how Chris and Neil were getting on.

The contact plan

The social worker, backed by one of the expert witnesses, argued that there should be no contact in this case. There was little evidence of emotional warmth during the meetings, and the parents struggled to engage with the children on their level. It was also the case that their brother Will demonstrated real trauma around attending contact, losing bowel control and being overwhelmed by anxiety.

The expert witness was specifically asked to report on contact matters, and noted that while the parents did love their children, there was no benefit to Chris or Neil from maintaining contact, but rather the opposite was true. He suggested that Neil's memories of home were coloured by images of neglect and abuse with associated feelings of insecurity and fear. It was felt that contact – even if indirect – would likely serve to remind him of these times, and it would be hard for Neil to reconcile these memories of abuse with the kindness associated with cards and gifts. In relation to Chris, it was acknowledged that while he would likely not be negatively impacted by contact, it would serve to separate him from Neil, and had the potential to undermine their sense of trust and security with each other.

There was an additional question about contact between the boys and their brother Will. At the time of preparing reports for the final court hearing, the social worker was suggesting that there should be no direct contact. Sadly, it was felt that the relationship between Will and Neil in particular was problematic, and the difficulties that Will demonstrated in his lack of empathy for others and bullying of younger children meant that any direct contact was difficult. Furthermore, the boys had been forced into sexual activity with each other that had distorted their relationship and left both boys feeling angry and confused. Following the last contact meeting, Will's carer had remarked that it had been nice to see Neil, and Will responded by going into a rage and smashing up furniture in his bedroom. It was decided that, given these issues, contact involving Will and his brothers needed to remain suspended pending some therapeutic work, but kept under review and considered again in the future.

Although there were other adults in the children's network, such as grandparents and aunts and uncles, it would appear that neither Chris nor Neil had close relationships with any of them, and it appeared that a number of these people had been involved in the sexual abuse of the boys. There was therefore no plan for contact with any of these family members.

CASE STUDY: AMANDA AND DEBBIE

Amanda and Debbie are white British children aged seven and five respectively. Until just over a year ago, they were living with their mother, Helen, at various addresses, including that of their maternal grandmother. Their father, Martin, has always lived locally, maintaining his own address, but often effectively living in the family home. The girls have four half-siblings, Steven, Jane, Joanne and Mark, who are all adults in their twenties. The girls have a particularly good relationship with their paternal grandfather and he put himself forward to care for them but was discounted on grounds of his poor health.

Helen and Martin have longstanding problem drug use, primarily heroin, and have made numerous efforts to address their addiction over the years; sometimes successfully for short periods, but always relapsing. There have also been numerous incidents of domestic violence, and Martin – who is diagnosed with a borderline personality disorder – is currently in prison for an attack on Helen. She has forgiven him, however, and visits regularly, making plans to be together when he is released.

Children's services have been involved on and off over the years with Amanda and Debbie regarding neglect, poor school attendance and concerns about their emotional well-being. Amanda has found herself in the role of carer for Debbie, and has also felt responsible for caring for her mother when she has been beaten up. Following the incident that resulted in Martin being imprisoned, interim care orders were granted by the court, and the plan for the girls is adoption.

The contact plan

When the girls came into care they were initially having a high level of contact with their mother, but Helen struggled to maintain her attendance, and when she did was often under the influence of heroin/

methadone. Contact was reduced, and eventually face-to-face contact was replaced with a weekly telephone call that appears to be working better, but requires the foster carer to telephone at different times until Helen answers and is in a position to speak with her daughters. When she is not under the influence of drugs, Helen is appropriate with the girls and conveys her love of them and desire for them to do well. Martin is having no contact at this time as he is in prison. Amanda and Debbie have a good understanding of their mother's "illness" and look forward to speaking with her, becoming upset if she is not available. Both say they "hate" Martin as he is "scary" and "hits Mummy".

Planning contact in this case is difficult for the social worker. Ideally, she would want the girls to have some sort of direct contact with their mother, preferably face-to-face, not least so that they did not worry about her or develop a fantasy about her being able to care for them, but she knows that Helen cannot be relied upon to maintain any consistency with plans. She also needs to balance the need for the girls to be reassured about Helen, with the need for them to settle with adoptive parents and focus on their own lives into the future. Any idea of achieving face-to-face contact is also made problematic by the fact that Helen and Martin will soon be reunited, and the girls do not want any contact with him. They have both witnessed some terrifying violence inflicted on their mother by him, and forcing them to see either him, or them both together, has the potential to re-traumatise them.

As a result of these factors, a decision was taken that face-to-face contact was not appropriate in this case, but that the girls' need for reassurance about their mother would be best met by having indirect letterbox contact once per year with three telephone contacts over the year initiated by the adopter. Plans were made to support the girls in participating, and also to actively support Helen in playing her part. It was agreed that Martin would not have contact as the girls did not want this.

Consideration was also given to contact plans with other relatives. It was noted that the girls' paternal grandfather had a particularly good relationship with them and when he was having contact as part of the viability assessment as a carer, the quality of warmth, affection and behaviour management was exemplary. The girls very much enjoyed their time with him, and it was therefore agreed that three contact meetings per year, with additional cards, presents and postcards, was in their interests. It was hoped that this might become less formal after the children were adopted so that he could play a relatively normal grandparent role for as long as his health allowed.

Sibling contact was not straightforward. The oldest sibling, Steven, had never really had much contact with the girls and, given that his current whereabouts were unknown, it was not possible to consider any contact. Mark was living independently, but had been convicted of a sexual assault on one of his other sisters. Linked with the fact that he had no relationship with Amanda or Debbie, this meant that contact was not deemed appropriate for him. Jane was a young adult with mild learning disabilities, who was living in supported accommodation but who spent most days visiting her mother's house. It was felt that she would not be able to maintain any independence from her mother or Martin, and could not make effective judgements about what to share and what not to share with Amanda and Debbie about the home situation. It was agreed that she would participate in Helen's letterbox contact.

Joanne's situation was slightly different in that she had achieved a level of independence from her birth family, although she still lived locally and had contact with them, and had achieved a stable lifestyle with a partner and young children. Joanne worked as a child care assistant in a day nursery and was being considered as a carer for her siblings until she withdrew, feeling that it would unreasonably impact on her immediate family. Joanne had indicated to the social worker that she would want to maintain contact with Amanda and Debbie if that was possible, and a plan for face-to-face contact meetings three times a year was agreed. The girls were very happy with this and the social worker felt it would help them maintain a link with their birth family, including their mother, but in a context where information and discussions would be sensitively filtered and presented in a child-centred way.

CASE STUDY: BAILEY

Bailey was removed from his birth family at the age of two as a result of concerns about his parents' alcoholism and resulting neglect. His birth parents had enough insight to acknowledge their failings and, although opposed to the adoption, did accept that this was the result of their own behaviour. Bailey's prospective adoptive parents demonstrated genuine empathy for his birth parents and were open to maintaining the contact, fully understanding the fact that he would always be connected to them.

The contact plan

Bailey was placed for adoption aged four years and one month, with a plan for face-to-face contact twice a year with both birth parents, and additional letterbox contact.

Bailey's birth parents needed a lot of support initially to accept the fact that he was legally and psychologically now a member of his new family, but they built up a degree of trust with the adopters and the adoption support worker. In the first couple of years, Bailey's adopters experienced the contact as beneficial for his development as he both wanted and needed to see them. Bailey was very concerned to see that his birth parents were well and safe and that they still loved him. Due to this need and the birth parents' commitment to adhering to the agreed plan, direct contact was a positive experience for all parties.

However, about two years into the placement, when Bailey was six, there was a noticeable change and Bailey's adopters reported that the last direct contact meeting had caused him a lot of emotional upset and they were questioning whether it was the right thing for him. Bailey had been asked for his view before the planned meeting, and he was very excited about the thought of it, but it was difficult to determine whether he was keen to see his birth parents because he really wanted to, or because he knew the day would consist of lots of attention, and time out of school to go somewhere fun. When asked if he had anything particular to ask his birth parents, he replied, 'No, I found out all I needed to know last year!'

Bailey's adopters told the adoption support worker that although they were prepared for him to be upset after contact, the most recent meeting had resulted in a longer-lasting negative impact. Since the meeting, Bailey's behaviour and emotions were "like a rollercoaster" with heightened anxiety levels and disturbed sleeping patterns including nightmares. There had been days where he was sobbing and crying, with high anxiety and worry. He was withdrawn and refused to discuss how he felt or what he was thinking. His adopters noted him being angry or very clingy and with a continuous need to be with at least one of them at all times; behaviours that were similar to when he first moved in with them.

Although Bailey was very bright, he was still only six years old, and the whole process of contact had appeared to open up old wounds, causing confusion and upset. Bailey's adopters tried to offer support and reassurance to him, but when they asked him about his feelings he refused to talk about his birth parents, saying 'It hurts too much and I don't want to talk about them'.

A decision was taken that Bailey should take a break from face-to-face contact and that this would be kept under review. Bailey had previously enjoyed seeing his birth parents and his reaction post-contact was not brought on by anything that they did or did not do on those specific days. Letterbox exchanges continued so that his birth parents could be reassured as to his well-being and Bailey would know he had not been forgotten. A great deal of work was invested in helping his birth parents accept that his adoptive parents were acting in Bailey's interests, not reneging on an agreement. The birth parents were saddened by this change but have accepted that Bailey's adoptive parents have his best interests at heart.

It was anticipated that as Bailey reached another developmental stage and, as he gained a more mature understanding of the circumstances that led to him being removed from their care, he would likely want to meet up with his birth parents again and would have more questions for them. However, at this point it was evident from his behaviour that the face-to-face contact was unsettling him and not promoting healthy development in the context of his adoptive home. What was a well thought out and appropriate contact plan that had worked well for two years needed to be reviewed and revised in light of emerging developments that could not have been predicted at the outset.

CASE STUDY: ALISHA

Alisha is a 15-year-old young woman of mixed heritage who was adopted at the age of five by a same sex couple – Sandra, who is of mixed ethnicity, and Erika, who is white German. Alisha's birth mother Brigit is white Irish and her birth father Stephen is black British, of Caribbean descent, and she has two paternal half-sisters who she has never met.

Alisha had initially come into care as the result of her mother's poor mental health that had meant she was unable to provide good enough care, and at times needed to be hospitalised for her own safety. Alisha's parents had separated by this time and her father was living with his new partner and their two small children. Stephen had wanted to take on the care of Alisha, but social work assessments concluded this was unrealistic given that his relationship was already under stress and he would be relying on his partner to do much of the child care. The court subsequently decided that adoption was the best plan for Alisha.

The contact plan

When planning contact Brigit was too unwell to participate, and so the plan simply recorded a need for letterbox contact annually, with an idea that this might need to be revisited subsequently. Stephen's contact with Alisha during care proceedings had always been of a high quality, but he had not worked well with social workers, feeling that he was being stereotyped as an absent father. At times his behaviour was perceived as being aggressive and threatening, and although he had very much wanted to maintain direct contact with Alisha after adoption, the plan was also for indirect letter box contact annually, and there were no arrangements made for any contact with Alisha's siblings.

For a number of years the adoption appeared to be working very well. Alisha settled quickly and formed good attachments with her new parents. She had an active lifestyle, enjoyed athletics and dance, had lots of friends and was doing well at school. Although the planned letterbox contact had not continued – largely because there had never been any response from either parent – Alisha gave no indication that she was troubled by her adoptive status.

Then, when Alisha was fourteen, with no warning or preparation, she received a Facebook message from her birth father, apologising for not having been in touch and saying that she was now old enough to decide for herself whether to have contact with him. Alisha was understandably shocked, excited and confused. She began communicating with him, and subsequently with her siblings, and was clear that she intended to develop and maintain a relationship with them. She had begun discussions about when she might visit them.

Although the content of Stephen's communication was not inappropriate, Alisha was struggling to manage the emotional disruption that his reintroduction into her life had brought. The timing in particular was unhelpful as Alisha had entered adolescence. She was questioning her identity in all respects, and she was just beginning to challenge her adoptive parent's authority in the way that teenagers typically do.

Alisha's school work began to deteriorate, and her behaviour at both school and home became more difficult. Increasingly she was spending time with more disruptive peers who she had previously described as "losers", and had become less committed to her dance and athletics. She was spending more and more time on Facebook – often late into the night – and had initiated an on-line search for her birth mother, albeit without success.

Sandra and Erika felt powerless to challenge what was happening. They had always been open to contact, although perhaps not as proactive as they might have been, and a little reluctant to bring up the past when things were going so well. They now tried to engage with Alisha to help her think through the consequences of her actions, but she was increasingly defiant and blaming them for the fact that her father had not been allowed contact with her during her early childhood. During arguments she was threatening to leave and return to her birth father.

The adopters contacted their agency for support and were visited by a social worker. In reviewing what had happened, it was felt that the original contact plans might have contributed to creating the current situation. It may have been that Stephen could have managed some direct contact from the time of the adoption onwards, as his interaction with Alisha had always been good. This might have helped Alisha to better integrate her past and present, and would have certainly meant that her birth father could not have re-entered her life in the way that he did. Sandra and Erika also accepted that they might have been more proactive in maintaining the planned indirect contact, possibly seeking the assistance of the adoption agency in working with both birth parents.

CASE STUDY: TYLER, ROSA AND JENNA

Rosa and Jenna, aged eight and five, are Black British children who have been living with their aunt Patricia on Interim Care Orders for about six months. They first became looked after two years ago as the result of neglect by their parents, Keta and Bernie, who have long-standing drug and alcohol problems. The children were initially placed with a stranger foster carer, with their 12-year-old brother Tyler, but he was quickly moved to another foster home because of his aggression towards his sisters.

The children's aunt Patricia is a Black British woman who lives with her husband Dexter, and her seven-year-old son Leon from a previous relationship. Patricia and Dexter are approved as kinship foster carers, but the plan is that they become Special Guardians for Rosa and Jenna. Although Keta and Bernie are currently abstaining from drugs and alcohol, this is very recent, and past evidence suggests they will struggle to maintain this for any length of time.

The contact plan

Rosa and Jenna are currently having weekly supervised contact with their birth parents and Keta and Bernie are arguing that they should be allowed to resume the care of their daughters. The quality of their contact has always been good when they are not under the influence of drugs or alcohol; the children look forward to seeing them, enjoy the sessions, but also leave happily when it is time to return to Patricia. Rosa and Jenna are also having contact once a week with Tyler who can be kind and engaging with them but also can call them cruel names and hit them when he thinks this behaviour will go unnoticed.

In making a contact plan as part of the proposal for Special Guardianship, the social worker was thinking that the girls should have direct contact with their parents and with Tyler three times per year, and that Patricia and Dexter should take responsibility for managing this. While Patricia had always been in favour of contact and understood that it was important for the girls to maintain positive relationships with their parents and brother, she was concerned about being given the responsibility for managing this.

Patricia was worried about Keta and Bernie's emotional state, knowing that contact would be difficult for them once the Special Guardianship Order was made, and it would potentially be distressing for the children if the adults were not coping. She was also concerned that Keta and Bernie had only been drug and alcohol free for a short period, and if they relapsed and arrived at contact intoxicated, she might struggle to protect the children without calling the police and creating a difficult situation. As a result, Patricia felt it was better that the contact meetings continued to be held in a neutral venue supervised by professionals who could offer support to the parents while she could be available to support the children, at least until matters were more settled.

Patricia further suggested to the social worker that the girls needed a staged reduction of contact after the Special Guardianship Order was made, rather than moving directly from weekly to three times per year, and that Keta and Bernie needed financial assistance for rail fares, as without this they might not attend and the children would be let down.

Patricia was also expected to contact Tyler's foster carer to arrange contact between them. When she had spoken to this carer by telephone she was told to 'bring the girls anytime ...Tyler was looking forward to seeing his sisters ....and they could all stay overnight if things were going well'. Patricia felt that she needed the arrangement to be more structured so that she could to prepare the girls, manage the risks, and maximise the chances of this contact being a success.

Patricia's concerns were so great that she contacted the children's social worker and the Children's Guardian, and said that she was having second thoughts about the placement because she was so worried about managing contact and the negative impact it might have on the girls. A meeting was called with all parties, and a revised contact plan was established that addressed Patricia's concerns. Patricia and Dexter were very relieved about this, and felt reasured that with appropriate support the family could help the children to have successful and safe contact with their parents.

Bibliography

Adoption Policy Review Group (2005), *Adoption: Better choices for our children, the report of Phase II*, Edinburgh: Scottish Executive, available at www.scotland.gov.uk at Publications, 29 June 2005.

Aldgate J (2009) *Living in Kinship Care: A child centred view*, Adoption & Fostering, 33:3, pp 51–63

Argent H (ed) (1995) *See You Soon: Contact with children looked after by local authorities*, London: BAAF

Argent H (ed) (2002) *Staying Connected: Managing contact in adoption*, London: BAAF

Argent H (2004) *What is Contact? A guide for children*, London: BAAF

Barker S, Beckett C, Borthwick S, Cullen D, Plumtree A and Spencer M (1999) *Contact in Permanent Placement*, London: BAAF

Barratt S and Granville J (2006) 'Kinship care: family stories, loyalties, and binds', in Kenrick J, Lindsey C and Tollemache L (eds) (2006) *Creating New Families: Therapeutic approaches to fostering, adoption and kinship care*, London: Karnac Books

Biehal N, Ellison S, Baker C and Sinclair I (2010) *Belonging and Permanence: Outcomes in long term foster care and adoption*, London: BAAF

Bond H (2007) *Ten Top Tips for Managing Contact*, London: BAAF

Brodzinsky D (2005) 'Reconceptualising openness in adoption: implications for theory, research and practice', in Brodzinsky D and Palacios J (eds) *Psychological Issues in Adoption: Research and practice*, New York, NY: Greenwood Press, pp 145–166

Cleaver H (2000) *Fostering Family Contact*, London: The Stationery Office

Department for Education (2011) *Family and Friends Care: Statutory guidance for local authorities*

Farmer E (2009) 'Making kinship care work', *Adoption & Fostering*, 33:3, pp 15–27

Farmer E and Moyers S (2008) *Kinship Care: Fostering effective family and friends placements*, London: Jessica Kingsley Publications

Foxon J (2003) *Nutmeg Gets a Letter*, London: BAAF

Fratter J (1996) *Adoption with Contact: Implications for policy and practice*, London: BAAF

Fratter J, Rowe J, Sapsford D and Thoburn J (1991) *Permanent Family Placement: A decade of experience*, London: BAAF

Fursland (2010) *Social Networking and Contact: How social workers can help adoptive families*, London: BAAF

Grotevant HD, McRoy RG and Ayres-Lopez S (2004) 'Contact after adoption: outcomes for infant placements in the USA', in Neil E and Howe D (eds) (2004) *Contact in Adoption and Permanent Foster Care: Research, theory and practice*, London: BAAF

Howe D and Feast J (2000) *Adoption, Search and Reunion: The long-term experience of adopted adults*, London: The Children's Society

Howe D and Steele M (2004) 'Contact in cases in which children have been traumatically abused or neglected by their birth parents', in Neil E and Howe D (eds) (2004) *Contact in Adoption and Permanent Foster Care: Research, theory and practice*, London: BAAF

Humphreys C and Kiraly M (2011) 'High-frequency family contact: a road to nowhere for infants', *Child & Family Social Work*, 16:1, pp 1–11

Hunt J, Waterhouse S, and Lutman E (2010) 'Parental contact for children placed in kinship care through care proceedings', *Child and Family Law Quarterly*, 22:1, pp 71–92

Kenrick J (2009) 'Concurrent planning: a retrospective study of the continuities and discontinuities of care, and their impact on the development of infants and young children placed for adoption by the Coram Concurrent Planning Project', *Adoption & Fostering*, 33: 4, pp 5–18

Lindsey C (2006) 'Contact with birth families: implications for assessment and integration in new families', in Kenrick J, Lindsey C and Tollemache L (eds) (2006) *Creating New Families. Therapeutic approaches to fostering, adoption and kinship care*, London: Karnac Books

Logan J and Smith C (2004) 'Direct post-adoption contact: experiences of birth and adoptive families', in Neil E and Howe D (eds) (2004) *Contact in Adoption and Permanent Foster Care: Research, theory and practice*, London: BAAF

Lowe N, Murch M, Borkowski M, Weaver A, Beckford V and Thomas C (1999) *Supporting Adoption: Reframing the approach*, London: BAAF

Loxterkamp L (2009) 'Contact and truth: the unfolding predicament in adoption and fostering', *Clinical Child Psychology and Psychiatry*, 14:3, pp 423–435

Macaskill C (2002) *Safe Contact: Children in permanent placement and contact with their birth relatives*, Lyme Regis: Russell House Publishing

Morgan R (2006) *About Adoption: A children's views report*, London: CSCI. Also available at: www.rights4me.org

Neil E (2002) 'Contact after adoption: the role of agencies in making and supporting plans', *Adoption & Fostering*, 26:1, pp 25–38

Neil E (2004a) 'The "Contact after Adoption" study: face-to-face contact', in Neil E and Howe D (eds) (2004) *Contact in Adoption and Permanent Foster Care: Research, theory and practice*, London: BAAF

Neil E (2004b) 'The "Contact after Adoption" study: indirect contact and adoptive parents' communication about adoption', in Neil E and Howe D (eds) (2004) *Contact in Adoption and Permanent Foster Care: Research, theory and practice*, London: BAAF

Neil E, Cossar J, Jones C, Lorgelly P and Young J (2011) *Supporting Direct Contact after Adoption*, London: BAAF

Neil E and Howe D (eds) (2004) *Contact in Adoption and Permanent Foster Care: Research, theory and practice*, London: BAAF

Performance and Innovation Unit (2000) *The Prime Minister's Review of Adoption*, London: Cabinet Office

Plumtree A (2011), *Permanence and Adoption for Children: A guide to the Adoption and Children (Scotland) Act 2007*, London: BAAF

Quinton D, Rushton A, Dance C and Mayes D (1997) 'Contact between children placed away from home and their birth parents: research issues and evidence', *Clinical Child Psychology and Psychiatry*, 2:3, pp 393–413

Roth D, Lindley B and Ashley C (2011) *Big Bruv Litle Sis*, London: Family Rights Group

Rowe J and Lambert L (1973) *Children Who Wait*, London: Association of British Adoption Agencies

Sants H J (1964) 'Genealogical bewilderment in children with substitute parents', *British Journal of Medical Psychology*, 37, pp 133–141

Schofield G and Simmonds J (2011) 'Contact for infants subject to care proceedings', Family Law, 41 (June), pp 617–22

Scottish Government (2011), *Guidance on the Looked After Children (Scotland) Regulations 2009 and the Adoption and Children (Scotland) Act 2007*, Edinburgh: Scottish Government, available at www.scotland.gov.uk at Publications, 10 March 2011

Selwyn J (2004) 'Placing older children in new families: changing patterns of contact', in Neil E and Howe D (eds) (2004) *Contact in Adoption and Permanent Foster Care: Research, theory and practice*, London: BAAF

Simmonds J (2011) *The Role of Special Guardianship: Best practice in permanency planning for children*, London: BAAF

Smith G (1995) 'Do children have a right to leave their pasts behind them? Contact with children who have been abused', in Argent H (ed) *See You Soon: Contact with children looked after by local authorities*, London: BAAF

Smith C and Logan J (2004) *After Adoption: Direct contact and relationships*, London: Routledge and Kegan Paul

Smith M, Bee P, Heverin A and Nobes G (1995) 'Parental control within the family: the nature and extent of parental violence to children', in Department of Health (ed) *Child Protection: Messages from research*, London: HMSO, pp 83–85

Thoburn J (2004) 'Post-placement contact between birth parents and older children', in Neil E and Howe D (eds) (2004) *Contact in Adoption and Permanent Foster Care: Research, theory and practice*, London: BAAF

Thomas C and Beckford V (1999) *Adopted Children Speaking*, London: BAAF

Triseliotis J (1973) *In Search of Origins*, London: Routledge and Kegan Paul

Triseliotis J (2010) 'Contact between looked after children and their parents: a level playing field?', *Adoption & Fostering*, 34:3, pp 59–66

Triseliotis J, Shireman J and Hundleby M (1997) *Adoption: Theory, policy and practice*, London: Cassell

Verrier N (2009) *The Primal Wound: Understanding the adopted child*, London: BAAF

Weise J (1987) *Trans-racial Adoption: A Black Perspective*, Norwich: University of East Anglia Monograph Series

Wellard S (2011) *Too Old to Care: The experiences of older grandparents raising their grandchildren*, London: Grandparents Plus

Young J and Neil E (2009) 'Contact after adoption', in Schofield G and Simmonds (eds) *The Child Placement Handbook: Research, Policy and Practice*, London: BAAF